IMAGES
of America

WALLINGFORD'S HISTORIC LEGACY

Looking through the eyes of this young boy at the corner of North Main and Center Streets evokes a nostalgia for days gone by. Through centuries of change and progress, Wallingford remains a community deeply rooted in its colonial past but continually striving to meet the needs of the present while preparing for the future. The "Uncle Sam Wants You" placard in front of the old post office exemplifies Wallingford's centuries-old fidelity to the nation and its steadfastness in answering the call of duty. (Courtesy of the Wallingford 350 Committee.)

On the Cover: This photograph was taken around 1942 in the business section of Wallingford and shows the stores from the corner of Center and North Orchard Streets across from the Center Street Cemetery. The brick block on the corner is Leighton's Block, which housed W.T. Grant, the Star Bowling Alley, and the pool rooms. Woolworth's 5 & 10, Fulton Market, Lacouciere's Paint Store, and Wolf's are also shown. (Courtesy of the Wallingford Historical Society.)

IMAGES
of America

WALLINGFORD'S HISTORIC LEGACY

Beth Devlin, Dawn Gottschalk,
and Tarn Granucci
Foreword by Bob Beaumont

ISBN 978-1-4671-0494-4

Published by Arcadia Publishing
Charleston, South Carolina

Printed in the United States of America

Library of Congress Control Number: 2019955569

For all general information, please contact Arcadia Publishing:
Telephone 843-853-2070
Fax 843-853-0044
E-mail sales@arcadiapublishing.com
For customer service and orders:
Toll-Free 1-888-313-2665

Visit us on the Internet at www.arcadiapublishing.com

To the founders, descendants, and citizens of Wallingford,
past, present, and future.

Contents

FOREWORD

During its first 350 years, Wallingford has been a truly remarkable town. It was the first interior village founded by the freemen of New Haven. John Moss Sr. and John Brockett Sr. were representatives to the Connecticut Colony's Court of Election in Hartford and traveled to and from Hartford on what would become part of the Old Boston Post Road in 1673. They found that the land between the New Haven and Hartford colonies made an ideal candidate for a new village.

Wallingford's citizens were always at the forefront of defending the town, colony, and country. From King Philip's War in the 1670s to sending men to help the British take Fort Louisburg in Nova Scotia, to serving in the French and Indian War, to being called the "Cradle of American Liberty" by the press in the 1760s, to providing over 10 percent of its population during the American Revolution, to the conflicts of the 20th and 21st centuries, this commitment to liberty has endured.

On another front, Wallingford was initially an area of 100 square miles but by 1774 was one of the largest towns in the colony, which included Cheshire and Meriden and the eastern districts of Prospect. In addition, one of her sons was the named proprietor in the founding of Wallingford, Vermont, in 1761, of which his son and other Wallingfordites became the early settlers.

As with all towns, it is the people who have made Wallingford what it was and has become. This includes the farmers, orchard men, industrialists, businesspeople, artists, musicians, and public servants. There has always been a broad base of creative, dedicated individuals who have given their all to the town. Those who have left their Wallingford roots and made names for themselves include one of the founders of the Associated Press and another who was instrumental in bringing Virginia back into the Union after the Civil War. But Wallingford is likely unique in that from the same founding family a signer of the Declaration of Independence was born here, while another descendant, although not born here, became the prime minister of the United Kingdom, not once, but twice. Wallingford is a typical New England town with a rich history, poised for a wonderful future.

—Bob Beaumont

ACKNOWLEDGMENTS

This book was produced for the celebration of Wallingford's 350 Jubilee. It is intended to give homage to Wallingford's founding fathers, some of its earliest families, and explore the foundations of Wallingford's success as a Puritan village in Colonial America. It is by no means a complete history of the town's past 350 years but rather an endeavor to explore some significant elements of Wallingford's past and share how they have influenced Wallingford's growth and development as an enduring New England town.

This book was a collaborative effort. So many have generously shared their passion for Wallingford history to make this book possible. Sincere thanks go to the Wallingford 350 Committee for their tireless assistance in providing support, photographs, and historical data for this project, including the 350 Moments of Wallingford history. In addition, this project could not have been produced without the generous help and support of the following institutions and individuals: Noma Beaumont and Pat and Ray Chappell of the Wallingford Historical Society; Jerry Farrell Jr., Bobbie Borne, and Mary Beth Applegate of the Wallingford Historic Preservation Trust; Wallingford Public Library; Bob Devaney; Choate Rosemary Hall archivists Judy Donald and Stephanie Gold; William Burgess; Roger Dietz; Larry Fishbein; Barbara Self; Robert Alexander Taber; Amy Humphries; Jean Saccavino Garcia; Alexandra Antonides-Kristjansson; Chelsea Smith-Antonides; and Scott Thurston. We wish to give a heartfelt thanks to Caroline Anderson at Arcadia Publishing for her advice and guidance. We are exceedingly grateful to Bob Beaumont of the Wallingford Historical Society for not only sharing his knowledge of history, but also for his generosity of spirit and time given to every aspect of this project. He is a true scholar of Wallingford history and a treasure to the community.

Unless otherwise noted, all images are courtesy of the Wallingford 350 Committee and its associated organizations.

Introduction

As Wallingford commemorates its 350-year jubilee, we look to the past to understand what inspired the founding fathers to journey across the Atlantic to begin a new life in an unknown land. These chapters explore the roots of Wallingford's earliest years as a fledgling colonial village to an innovative capital of the silver manufacturing industry in the 19th century.

The 1630s brought tens of thousands of English citizens to the shores of the New World, attracted by not only religious freedom from the crown, but also by the seemingly endless economic possibilities. The colonists varied from indentured servants to tradespeople and wealthy speculators.

In 1637, Oxford-educated Rev. John Davenport was on the run from the religious prejudices imposed by the Church of England. Confident that greater opportunities lay across the sea, he and his childhood friend Theophilus Eaton recruited friends and colleagues and chartered a ship to set sail to the thriving and established Massachusetts Colony. With families and fellow Puritans in tow, they braved the weeks-long journey across the rough seas of the Atlantic with the aim of establishing business ventures and practicing the purest form of their religion. Each had hopes of settling in a new community with shared religious beliefs that offered the opportunity to obtain land and a bit of wealth along the way.

The group landed in Boston in June 1637. Upon arrival, Davenport and his traveling companions, mainly Londoners, were heralded as one of the wealthiest and most educated groups the Massachusetts colonists had seen to date. They noted that the new colonists were "gentleman in wealth and character, with their servants and household effects."

They spent nine months within the colony attempting to assimilate to the challenges and differences of the New World, deeply disappointed in the theological aberrations that greeted them and unnerved by the religious tension that permeated the colony. As a result, they decided to fund an expedition to explore farther along the coast with the hope of finding lands for the establishment of a new village.

The group notified the leaders in Boston of their plans to depart. In turn, the colony attempted to entice the group to stay by offering important positions within the community. Eaton's brother Nathaniel accepted an offer to become the first headmaster at the Boston colony's newly formed college, the future Harvard University. However, the majority of the group explained that as they were Londoners, most of them were not suited for a farming lifestyle, their differences were too great to stay within the colony, and they hoped to form a trading venture, seaport, and market town elsewhere.

Encouraged by reports that land was available for purchase farther west, Davenport, Eaton, and a small number of followers sailed from Boston. Three weeks later, they discovered a cozy harbor with farmland to the north and a multitude of rivers and streams. It had perfect proximity to the trading port of New Amsterdam and the Connecticut Colony in Hartford. Eaton and Davenport decided that this was the ideal spot to build their new community. Thus, New Haven was founded in 1638 and soon became a thriving trade town. They swiftly drew 500 members from the Massachusetts Colony and nearby villages and 30 years later became the birthplace of the future plantation of Wallingford.

New Haven Colony's second purchase of Native American land on December 11, 1638, included a tract 13 miles long and 10 miles wide along the Quinnipiac River. This land remained unsettled until after the Charter of 1662, when New Haven Colony was absorbed into the Connecticut Colony. This spurred some of its residents to look north with thoughts of venturing out once again in search of new opportunities.

The lands around the Quinnipiac River offered a wealth of potential, with streams and ponds for fishing, and forests for hunting. The colonists hoped to expand their farming prospects and continue to uphold their religious practices and beliefs. On board with the new venture were some of New Haven's most senior and distinguished residents, including John Moss Sr. and Nathaniel Merriman Sr., each of whom had signed the original New Haven covenant, and Thomas Yale, cousin of Elihu Yale, the namesake of the future Yale University. John Brockett had laid out the original settlement of New Haven, and was tasked with designing and allocating the first plots in the new village, which they would name Wallingford, meaning "old fortification" or "walled town," as a nod to Wallingford, England.

The new Wallingford Covenant was signed in 1669, and once again the colonists were on the move. With John Moss Sr. as its oldest member, supplies were loaded onto flat boats and oxen and the group headed north along the sandy plains of the Quinnipiac River. Included were the families of Samuel Hall, John Beach, Joseph Ives, Samuel Munson, Simon Tuttle, Abraham Doolittle, Samuel Cook, John Peck, and Samuel Street. Wallingford was born.

When planning for a new and independent village in the wilderness, which was fraught with dangers known and imagined, the early planters had to consider all of the elements needed to build a successful community. Beyond the practicalities of housing, clearing land, establishing a meetinghouse, building roads, and finding sustenance, they had to carefully consider the people and skills needed to survive. Communities depend on those who lead, those who teach, those who provide comfort and hope, those who protect, those who bring innovation and growth, and those who preserve their history. Their very survival depended on this symbiotic relationship.

As the world changed around it and the centuries passed and as the population grew, Wallingford rose to each new challenge. Schools grew from the humble one-room schoolhouse to multiple educational opportunities, both public and private. Dusty and mud-caked roads became trolley lines and then modern highways. Wallingford became a thriving agricultural center, and its second and third generations of children enjoyed the fruits of their ancestors' labor, becoming merchants, skilled tradespeople, industrialists, educators, and clerics. The influx of money enabled the colonists to form numerous ventures to the Ohio Western Reserve and present-day Vermont, where they formed new towns and settlements, some bearing the ancient names of Wallingford's founding families.

From the very beginning, Wallingford rejoiced in its success and mourned together during its painful losses. It commemorated milestones with much pomp and circumstance through parades, pageants, costume balls, reenactments, and ceremonies. Memorials for war, founding fathers, and historic events are scattered throughout the community. Wallingford's earliest town clerks carefully recorded the rigors of colonial life and its day-to-day challenges and concerns. Historians wrote lengthy tomes outlining the genealogies of the oldest families and provided details of the lives of the first residents. Societies formed, protecting and preserving memories, architecture, and artifacts.

Over the centuries, the founders' progeny wove in and out of each other's lives and through each other's family trees. Generation after generation, they worked shoulder to shoulder, supporting one another during fruitful days as well as the dark chapters of our nation's history. The earliest descendants produced copious amounts of children and continued to populate Wallingford for centuries, passing land, fortune, and skills from one generation to the next. Their primary focus remained true to the founders' earliest dreams: to live a peaceful life, establish businesses and farms, expand their land, and protect their faith and their freedom.

Throughout Wallingford, many streets and businesses continue to bear the names of the first settlers. Many of these very names left an enduring legacy of bravery, innovation, fortitude, and perseverance. These are the threads that connect our past to our present.

WALLINGFORD COVENANT

We whose names are underwritten being accepted by the committee of New Haven for ye intended village as planters and desiring that the worship and ordinances of God, may in due time, be set up and encouraged among us, as the main concernment of a Christian people, promise and engage ourselves that we shall not neither directly nor indirectly do any thing to hinder or obstruct any good means that shall be used by the said Committee or others instructed by them to promote the premises by securing a godly and able ministry among us to dispense the word of God; and when such ministry or a church of Christ shall be settled among us, we engage by no means to disturb the same in their choice of minister or ministers or other church officers or other of their ch'h rights, liberties or administrations, nor shall refuse or withdraw due maintenance from such minister or ministry, and further we do engage ourselves peaceably to submit to such settlement and Civil order as the said Committee shall direct among us either by themselves or some others as a committee but them appointed, upon the place, until the said village came to be an orderly establishment within itself; and lastly we doe engage personally to settle upon the place May next come twelve months, if God's providence inevitably hinder not, and observe and perform all and every the other articles agreed upon.

FOUNDING FATHERS

Samuel Street • Abraham Doolittle • John Brockett • Samuel Andrews • Samuel Hall
Nathaniel How • Joseph Ives • Samuel Munson • John Miles • Simon Tuttle
James Heaton • Benjamin Lewis • Thomas Hall • Jehiel Preston • Nathaniel Merriman
Samuel Cook • Joseph Benham • William Johnson • John Peck • Nathan Andrews
Samuel Miles • Daniel Hopper • Thomas Curtiss • John Beach • John Mosse
Jeremiah How • John Hall • Zachariah How • Samuel Potter • Eliazur Peck
Samuel Brown • John Ives • John Harriman • Samuel Whitehead
Thomas Yale • Eliazur Holt • Eliasaph Preston • Daniel Sherman

One

Colonial Years

Wallingford's first 30 years, from 1670 to 1700, were industrious and fruitful. Land was cleared, houses were built, and farmland was distributed to the colonists based on their rank in the village. With the goal of keeping peace within the town, they adopted a policy of exclusivity. No one could move into the colony without approval from the leaders. They cobbled together a society of friends and neighbors from New Haven, all bringing various skills and trades that would benefit the entire community.

The colonists lived an artisanal and agricultural lifestyle, marked by the rhythms of the seasons. They had abundant harvests in the fall and gave thanks for the fruits of their labor. Winters were long and growing seasons were short, making for difficult springs that brought want and deprivation.

Colonists shared every duty of the new plantation, from building homes and mills together to trading and bartering for critical supplies. Clothes were woven, cattle tended to, fields were cleared, houses built, and crops of flax and corn were planted. It was grueling work, but they had a shared vision to provide a foundation for future generations.

Aside from tending to their own farms and homes, each member contributed to the daily function of the community. Committees were formed to address all the needs of the village. Teachers were selected, taxes were collected, and arrangements were made to administer to the poor. Sheep masters, fence viewers, branders, watch duty, and the "beating of the drum" were highly prized responsibilities and were often rewarded with money or land. The most senior leaders were sent to the Connecticut Colony in Hartford to represent the village in all of its affairs.

During Wallingford's first decades, the settlers joined forces to protect each other from every conceived danger. Hundreds of wolves roamed the land, threatening cattle and sheep. Although the colonists enjoyed friendly trading and shared farmland with Native Americans, rumors of potential attacks kept them on their toes, necessitating round-the-clock guard duty of the village. When King Philip's War broke out in 1675, Wallingford was on high alert. Muskets were carried to church, houses were fortified, and guards watched over the precious gunpowder and supplies. Of the 40 men living in the village, eight were dutifully sent to the cause, illustrating the patriotism that would weave through the next three centuries. Nathaniel Merriman Jr. was the first resident to be lost in battle during the Great Swamp Fight in Rhode Island in 1675. Wallingford, unlike many New England villages, was spared invasion and deadly attacks during this bloody campaign, and its inhabitants lived in relative peace.

However, there were unexpected controversies and tragedies that arose. From 1647 to 1697, approximately 38 people were accused of witchcraft in Connecticut, and Wallingford was not spared from the mass hysteria. John and Joan Carrington were the first couple to be hanged in

Connecticut for accusations of witchcraft. They died in Wethersfield in 1651. Descendants of the Carringtons included Desire Carrington Munson Stanley, who was first married to Medad Munson, great-grandson of founder Samuel Munson, and later to Oliver Stanley Esq. of the Squire Stanley House. Winifred Benham, wife of Wallingford founder Joseph Benham, and their daughter 13-year-old Winifred Benham Jr. were accused and then later acquitted of witchcraft in 1697, during the last witch trial in the Connecticut Colony. The Tuttle family had two notable tragedies in the 17th century. Founder Simon Tuttle's brother Benjamin killed their sister Sara with an axe in 1676. Benjamin was hanged for his crime. Simon Tuttle's younger sister Mercy was married to fellow Wallingford founder Samuel Brown, grandson of founder John Brockett. In 1691, Mercy Tuttle Brown murdered her son Samuel Jr. with an axe, claiming that her crime was committed at the "instigation of the devil." She was tried, found guilty, and held in the custody of the magistrates in New Haven until her death three years later.

As Wallingford began to sprawl farther into the wilderness, farmers residing on the outskirts of town found that traveling to the village for Sunday Sabbath was much too cumbersome. These outlying farmers petitioned to have their own parishes, resulting in the towns of Cheshire and Meriden, and began to develop their own identities and communities.

Much like the century before it, the 1700s were punctuated by political upheaval and war, and Wallingford residents found themselves in the center of it all. In 1754, Wallingford men left their farms and families to serve in the French and Indian War, where they were richly rewarded with land grants in what is now known as Vermont. There they formed towns in the names of their ancestors. They returned home by 1763, now seasoned soldiers. Soon, the colonists found themselves thrust into the middle of a new war brewing between patriots and loyalists to the crown of England.

Wallingford's role in the Revolutionary War was extensive, with its citizens forming their own chapter of the Sons of Liberty and voting to defy the Stamp Act. They had a fully trained militia and a large supply of munitions, which the townspeople closely guarded. Fearful that the resident Tories would blow up their supplies, they were forced to place some of their own villagers under house arrest. Citizens turned against one another, and family loyalties were challenged. However, throughout the chaos of war, Wallingford residents made an impressive effort to collect supplies for their militia, from clothes and bedding to cooking utensils and tents. They sent troops to Boston, White Plains, Princeton, and Yorktown. At the end of the Revolutionary War in 1783, and over the next 100 years, Wallingford rose to become one of the leaders in America's Industrial Revolution.

The colonial history of Wallingford is revealed in part through the numerous 18th-century homes built by the grandsons of the original colonists and carefully preserved over the centuries. Center Street Cemetery contains the ancient headstones of the men and women whose stories have not been forgotten.

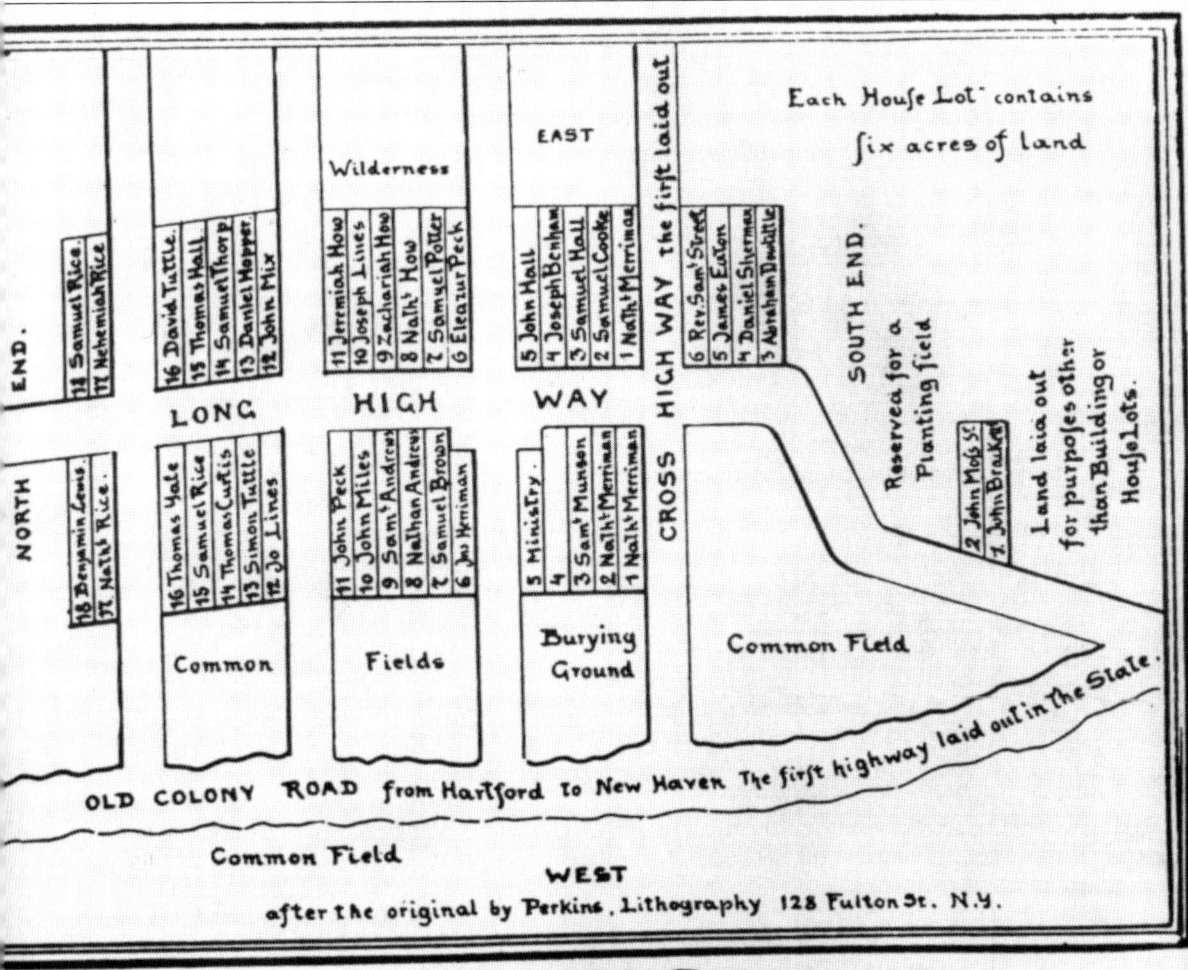

Pictured here is the first plot of Wallingford from around 1670. Founder John Brockett was tasked with plotting the new village and was responsible for assigning land to the new colonists. Six-acre parcels were awarded, and each had space for a dwelling and pastures to grow crops and for cattle to graze. The homes were located on the Long Highway on a ridge running north to south. Each house had a view of the Blue Hills and the sandy plains that swept west to the Quinnipiac River. The village included common pastures, a burying ground, a meeting house, and a parade ground where the militia would train. Additional land was assigned on the outskirts of the village and along the Quinnipiac River for the purpose of farming. During Wallingford's first decades, the colonists preferred to keep their dwellings close to one another in the center of town for safety, while they fortified the village against potential attacks.

John Moss was one of the founders of the New Haven Colony. He was deputy to the court of election in Hartford and a corporal in the train band, which was organized to help protect the colony from any form of attack. This training prepared him for duty in King Philip's War, where he served as a corporal. Moss was one of the first New Haven colonists to set his sights on establishing the new plantation in Wallingford, 12 miles north, and became one of the oldest signers of the Wallingford Covenant. Being a senior member of the new town, he was selected to supervise and manage the affairs of Wallingford and performed the town's first wedding. He died in 1707 at the age of 103 as Wallingford's first centenarian.

One of the earliest planters of Wallingford was Nehemiah Royce, born in 1636. His first plot of land was on the north end of town. Soon after his arrival, Royce went to work building his home. The Royce brothers' skills as carpenters were important to the new town, and they built one of the first gristmills and laid the foundation of the first church. Local legend claims that when Royce's two-story saltbox-style home was under construction, a storm unceremoniously knocked it over to the east. Royce, with assistance from his brothers and probably under great pressure to provide shelter, never completely straightened the house, causing it to lean to one side for the next 200 years. It was from Royce's large elm tree on the Long Highway that citizens kept watch for potential invasions. The original portion of the Royce House was built in 1671 and attached to the saltbox home pictured here.

Giles Hall was born in Wallingford in 1733. His great-grandfather was Rev. Samuel Street, who was Wallingford's first minister and founder, and he was also descended from founder John Hall. Brothers Giles, Lyman, and Street Hall were raised in Wallingford during the years prior to the Revolutionary War. In the mid-18th century, the lives of the Hall brothers took very different paths. Lyman made his mark in politics, Street became a revolutionary, and Giles led a comparatively quiet life. His father built him a large house on South Elm Street (pictured) in 1760. There, he raised a family, spent his life tending to his extensive farms, and occupied the house until his death in 1789. (Courtesy of William Burgess.)

The Giles Hall House on South Elm Street has many interesting elements that illustrate early colonial life. Extensively preserved, it contains features such as a birthing room, corner cupboards, a secret passageway between each bed chamber, and original glass in many of the windows. The home also features multiple fireplaces and a beehive oven. A massive stone chimney in the center of the house reaches from the cellar to the third-floor attic. The chimney is the heart of the house and provides architectural structure. Ancient bits of straw and horsehair are embedded in the chimney mortar. In the large attic, the chimney also features a smokehouse, which was utilized by colonial cooks to hang meat for curing. In colonial times, corn husks, horsehair, and corncobs were used for insulation. (Courtesy of William Burgess.)

Lyman Hall was born in Wallingford in 1724. He studied theology at Yale College and later studied medicine with a doctor in the Stratford-Fairfield area, eventually practicing in Sunbury, Georgia. In addition, he represented Georgia at the Second Continental Congress. On August 2, 1776, at the age of 52, Hall became one of the signers of the Declaration of Independence. In 1779, as British troops were invading New Haven, Sunbury was burned to the ground by British forces, and Hall fled with his family back to Connecticut. As the British retreated and relative peace came to the colonies, Hall returned to Georgia, where he was elected governor. Although he never picked up arms in defense of Wallingford, his policies and beliefs affected the colonies, and he made successful strides to rebuild Georgia after the revolution. This cenotaph honoring Lyman Hall is at the Center Street Cemetery.

Theophilus Jones was born in 1690 and moved to Wallingford in 1711. His grandfather was one of the first settlers of New Haven. He built his home (right) on Jones Road, southwest of town. The homestead contains a woodshed, pigeon house, icehouse, and carpentry shop, exemplifying life in colonial times. The John Barker home (below) was built in 1756 on Clintonville Road and is one of the oldest brick homes in Connecticut. Jones and Barker, both successful farmers with extensive landholdings, were among the several Wallingford families that owned slaves. (Both, courtesy of William Burgess.)

The Cook House was built in 1758 by Thaddeus Cook. Cook was a descendant of Wallingford founder Samuel Cook and was a colonel in the Revolutionary War, serving under General Gates in the Saratoga Campaign in 1777. Cook Hill Road was named for this renowned colonial family. (Courtesy of William Burgess.)

The Porter Cook House was built at 38 North Elm Street in 1789. In his diary of 1789, Porter Cook wrote of the raising of his new home, which demonstrates the community efforts of colonial life in Wallingford: "Samuel Doolittle of Pond Hill hued and framed the house, and Timothy Carrington and his son Lemuel clapboarded and shingled the house." (Courtesy of William Burgess.)

The only reminder of the life and service of Revolutionary War patriot Eliakim Hall is his ancient headstone at the Center Street Cemetery. During the war, Colonel Hall, who was uncle to the Hall brothers Lyman, Giles and Street, served with Col. Ethan Allen at the capture of Fort Ticonderoga and was also elected to lead the Committee of Inspection in Wallingford. The committee's top priority was to inquire into all cases of suspected loyalty to the crown and to "take proper measures." They identified several Wallingford Loyalists, whose properties were then confiscated. Prisoners including Benjamin Franklin's son William, the deposed royal governor of New Jersey, were held at times at the old Carrington House if they were suspected of loyalism. Eliakim Hall added to the family's wealth in 1761 when he was granted a six-mile square tract of land in Vermont. The land grant was divided among not only Eliakim Hall and his family, but among 60 fellow Wallingford citizens. A new town was developed and was duly named Wallingford, Vermont.

Street Hall's military career began in the French and Indian War (1754–1763). After the call for troops to Lexington, Colonel Hall organized troops from Wallingford and the surrounding towns and spent autumn of 1775 and winter of 1776 in Boston on Winter Hill in charge of the command. New Haven was considered an important supply town and was raided in July 1779 by British troops as a strategic move against the Continental army. According to the *Papers of the New Haven Colony Historical Society*, from Wallingford, Colonel Hall "rode over hills and through valleys at a furious pace," shouting "Turn out! Turn out! The British are in New Haven!" Seventy-six men from Meriden and 37 men from Wallingford followed Hall into battle, led by his cousin Capt. Caleb Hall. There they were joined by the New Haven militia, composed in part of 70 students from Yale College, about half the student population. New Haven citizens also participated in hand-to-hand combat, trying to push the British out of town. Street Hall became known as the "Terror of the Tories" and developed into a "fiery patriot and brave soldier," according to Charles Samuel Hall's *Hall Ancestry*. His grave can be found at Center Street Cemetery.

Two

THE 19TH CENTURY

By the early 1800s, the American colonies had achieved independence from England, Connecticut had its own constitution in 1818, and Wallingford had grown back to a population of 2,325 people after Cheshire (1780) and Meriden (1806) became their own towns. In an 1811 report to Connecticut's Academy of Arts & Sciences, George Washington Stanley commented on the state of Wallingford, observing every aspect of the town, including the success of the educational system, and the overall health of the economy. In Stanley's report, it was also worth noting that "females of mature years gathered in small and social groups for afternoon and evening parties" and "of the men, a large proportion possess a social and friendly disposition." Wallingford, after a grueling century of struggle to build a solid foundation, was finally transitioning to a new era where the citizenry had finally gained a little time for pleasant diversion. Stanley also stated that Wallingford had a library, established in 1791, with over 217 volumes, and that a "Society for the purpose of mutual improvement in useful knowledge" was formed in 1810 with 50 members, evidence that Wallingford was striving to cultivate enlightenment within its society.

Wallingford was thriving, and old colonial names such as Yale, Hall, Pomeroy, and Carrington were producing everything from Britannia housewares and wagon wheels to coffee mills throughout town. Their original success in agriculture was due in large part to their trading enterprises throughout the colonies. This wealth enabled farmers to expand into manufacturing, and their proximity to the coast of New Haven enabled them to expand shipping enterprises as far as the West Indies. During this new prosperity and success, Connecticut's borders and economy were threatened again when Pres. James Madison declared war against Great Britain in June 1812.

The British navy was aggressively patrolling the East Coast and Long Island Sound and virtually closed the Atlantic trade routes. Fearing a devastating impact on trade, the War of 1812 was unpopular with Connecticut residents. However, Wallingford dutifully responded with men and supplies, sending soldiers to Fort Griswold to defend New London and the Thames River from the British. The British blockade deeply affected shipping on Long Island Sound; however, it stimulated rapid growth in the manufacturing industry as Wallingford rallied to produce goods it could no longer import.

Wallingford began to experience an industrial revolution. Dozens of enterprises were formed under the names of Wallingford's first families. The beauty of Wallingford's landscape, the power of the Quinnipiac River, and the prosperity of its people attracted innovators in business and industry. With this achievement came social reform and philanthropy.

Robert Wallace introduced German silver to Wallingford manufacturing, and Samuel Simpson began experimenting with electroplating silver onto metal home goods, both of which produced an industry that would create hundreds of jobs and, in turn, introduce a wave of European immigrants seeking work. As the diversity of Wallingford's citizens grew, so did the expanse of housing, churches, and schools. In 1808, Yalesville was named in honor of the Charles Yale family whose Britannia ware factories were instrumental in the growth of Wallingford manufacturing.

Moses Yale Beach, founder of the *New York Sun* newspaper, returned to Wallingford in 1851 and built a large Italianate mansion on North Main Street. He was an enthusiastic supporter of Wallingford's educational system.

One of Wallingford's many influential families of the era was that of Samuel Simpson. Simpson came from an old Wallingford farming family, and with the introduction of his successful silver manufacturing company, Simpson, Hall, Miller & Company in the mid-1800s, came enormous wealth that he readily shared throughout the community. His philanthropy was extended to the public school system, the water works development, and to St. Paul's Episcopal Church, to which he donated $25,000 for its reconstruction in 1868.

In the middle of Wallingford's industrial success came the American Civil War, and Wallingford braced itself for yet another era of sorrow and disruption. Between 1861 and 1865, the town sent 228 men to fight for the cause. Silver manufacturers provided use of their buildings to house troops and converted their factories to produce war provisions. Moses Yale Beach's good works continued; he installed a 110-foot-tall Liberty Pole on Main and Center Streets and donated $100,000 to support the Union army. By the end of the war, Wallingford's silver manufacturing continued to grow to meet demands for affordable home goods and hollowware.

Wallingford made major advancements in public services during the 19th century, improving transportation and modernizing utilities. The Wallingford Water Company was formed in 1881 and brought Wallingford's water supply from Lake Pistapaug, east of town. By the fall of 1889, eighteen miles of pipeline were maintained throughout town. The Wallingford Gas Light Company was formed in 1883, providing streetlights. And by 1886, crushed stone paved the roads, and 20 miles of concrete sidewalks were laid. Transportation grew from horse and carriage to trolleys and trains, including the Airline passenger railroad on the east side of Airline Road, east of town. Large commercial buildings first made their appearance in 1857, one of which housed Wallingford's first opera house and a variety of merchants. Wallingford gained its first bank, the Dime Savings Bank, founded in 1871.

By the end of the 19th century, evidence of Wallingford's success could be found up and down Main Street. Industrialists had accumulated great wealth in the wake of the Civil War, and as small backyard factories moved west to the shores of the Quinnipiac River, large homes were built by some of Wallingford's most successful business owners. Victorian-era mansions, ornate gardens, and towering elm trees lined the streets, and societies to "beautify" the town were formed. Although more than a few mansions were built in the mid-19th century, most of the architecture reflected the restrained sensibilities of the descendants of Wallingford's founders, whose Puritan ethics were passed down from generation to generation.

By the late 19th century, much of Wallingford's early industries left the center of town and moved to the Quinnipiac River to the west. Wallingford's primary thoroughfare was originally named the Long Highway; however, the name was changed to Main Street by the 19th century. Many streets bear the names of some of the oldest residents, and some are descriptive of the land that the roads were built upon. Rembert Street was named for Stephen Rembert, who once owned the Simpson House, and Orchard Street was thus named as it crossed through the Moses Beach orchards. This aerial photograph shows downtown Wallingford. Choate Rosemary Hall campus is at upper right, and the distinctive cupola of the Moses Beach Mansion is at bottom right.

The intersection of Main and Center Streets has been the heart of Wallingford since 1670. In the 18th century, enterprising citizens manufactured a wide variety of goods from their homes and outbuildings right along Main Street. The Carringtons manufactured coffee mills on East Center Street, and the Yales produced Britannia goods on the corner of South Main Street. Everything from shoes, coffins, wheels, razor strops, and beaver hats were produced. During the 19th century, as private manufacturing left for the rivers and streams for larger production, the town reflected a more genteel era. Trees were planted, sidewalks were installed, and trolley cars carried passengers up and down the streets. Main Street is seen here facing north near Center Street.

By the middle of the 19th century, Wallingford's economy was booming, and there was a great need for more commercial space within its town center. Merchants welcomed two large developments in town that would provide office space and storefronts. The Simpson Block, above, was commissioned by Samuel Simpson, the town's leading industrialist, in 1887. Constructed of brick and four stories tall, it was an imposing structure. In 1895, it housed C.N. Lane's large store, which carried newspapers, toys, stationery, and tobacco. It also held George Wilkinson's opera house. The William Wallace Block at 33 North Main Street, below, was built in 1857, before the onset of the Civil War. It was one of Wallingford's first commercial buildings, and was commissioned by William Wallace, a local real estate developer.

Moses Yale Beach, born in Wallingford in 1800, was the only son of Moses Sperry Beach and Lucrecia Yale. One of Beach's notable ancestors was Elihu Yale, governor of the East India Company and namesake of Yale University. In 1835, Beach moved to New York City, where he purchased a newspaper, the *Sun*, which would become the most successful penny paper in the city. Beach realized that one of the difficulties of publishing the news was the inability to report it in a timely fashion. With the invention of the telegraph, it became possible to receive dispatches quickly, but it was costly. Beach and other New York papers pooled their resources to share telegraphic messages. This collaboration was the foundation of the Associated Press. By the early 1840s, the *Sun* held the largest circulation in the world, publishing not only the news of the day, but stories written by budding author Edgar Allen Poe. With his paper a firm success, Beach retired at age 48, handing over the *Sun* to his children Moses S. Beach and Alfred Ely Beach. This photograph shows Moses Yale Beach with his second wife, Julia Beach. (Courtesy of the Smithsonian digital archives.)

Divorced from his first wife, Nancy Day Beach, Moses Beach returned to his hometown of Wallingford with his second wife, Julia. He settled into Wallingford society, using his fortune to build the stately Beach Mansion on North Main Street, designed by New Haven architect Henry Austin. Moses Yale Beach lived a quiet life; however, he was generous with his fortune, bestowing gifts where needed. In 1861, at the onset of the Civil War, Wallingford was gathering its young men to join the fight. At a town meeting, officials received a patriotic letter from Beach offering to assist the war effort by donating $100,000 to outfit their company of volunteers and to provide a flag and liberty pole. Over 50 men enrolled at once, and after the meeting adjourned, the volunteers marched to the Beach Mansion and serenaded him from below. Beach died in 1868, and his mansion was demolished in 1960.

As a child, Moses Beach had a talent for mechanics and often created toys for his schoolmates. At age 14, he asked to be apprenticed to a cabinet maker in Hartford. There he learned a trade and developed a work ethic and determination that became the foundation of his future success. He bargained with his master for additional work and at 18 years of age had saved enough money to buy his freedom from the contract, enabling him to form his own cabinetmaking business in Northampton, Massachusetts. He was honored for his cabinet work (pictured) by the Agricultural and Domestic Manufacturers Society at the age of 21. Beach spent his early years in the pursuit of inventions, such as an engine for boat travel and a rag-cutting machine of the type used for the next 100-plus years.

Dr. Jared Potter Kirtland was born in Wallingford in 1793 and was the grandson of the famed Dr. Jared Potter of Wallingford. Kirtland enrolled in the newly established Yale Medical School at Yale College in 1812. After graduation, he married Caroline Atwater, daughter of Joshua Atwater, and began a medical practice, first in Wallingford, then in Durham. Dr. Kirtland then moved his family to Ohio's Western Reserve and joined the multitude of other Wallingford natives who helped found many of the towns in western Ohio, including Atwater. Dr. Kirtland practiced botany, was a noted naturalist, cofounded the Western Reserve College Medical School, and founded the Cleveland Museum of Natural History. (Courtesy of the Wallingford Historical Society.)

Samuel Simpson was born in Wallingford in 1814. He began his career at 18 years old as an apprentice to Charles Yale in the manufacturing of Britannia goods. He soon became a pioneer in the manufacturing of Britannia, nickel, silver, and silver-plated housewares. Although he held the position of president of Simpson, Hall, Miller & Company and of the Simpson Nickel Silver Company, he was noted throughout Wallingford for his humility and kindness and was described by historian William Richard Cutter as a "best friend to the poor and unfortunate." Simpson's legacy lives on through the many charitable causes he devoted his life to. The Wallingford Public Library, the Wallingford Fire Department, Simpson Court, St. Paul's Episcopal Church, and the parks and public school system are all benefactors of his good will and devotion. His generosity and contributions reach far beyond his century, and his indelible mark can be seen throughout Wallingford. (Courtesy of the Wallingford Historical Society.)

At the age of 53, Samuel Simpson purchased a modest Greek Revival home on Main Street (pictured) from Stephen Rembert, a South Carolina plantation owner. The property ran all the way to Colony Road and commanded some of the most spectacular views in Wallingford. He quickly retained New Haven architect Henry Austin to design a complete remodel of the house. Although the house was built around 1840 by John Meigs Hall, some of the structural beams dated to the 1600s, as they once were part of an older dwelling constructed on that very spot by Joseph Holt. The house stayed within the Simpson family until the 1980s. The Simpson Taber House was then sold and removed to Scard Road on the east side of town to make room for the new Wallingford library. Simpson's daughter Martha kept detailed journals of her life in the Simpson house in the 1800s, noting that most evenings were spent welcoming frequent visitors and playing the Victorian parlor game whist. Samuel Simpson often held his company board meetings in the house, and the family lounged on the expansive porches overlooking their extensive rose gardens and the bustling Main Street.

Arthur Henry Dutton was born in Wallingford on November 15, 1838. After attending Yale College, he went to West Point Military Academy. In June 1861, he graduated third in his class of 35 as a member of the engineer corps. (In the same graduating class was Cadet George Custer, who graduated at the opposite end of the class rankings and later led the most ferocious battle of the Sioux Wars—the Battle of Little Bighorn, also known as Custer's Last Stand.) In 1862, Dutton had become commander of the 3rd Brigade in the 3rd Division of the 9th Army Corps during the Civil War. By May 1864, for services rendered at the Battle of Drewry's Bluff on May 16, Dutton was promoted to colonel in the US Army and brigadier general of the Connecticut Volunteers. On May 26 at Bermuda Hundred, while leading a reconnoitering mission with his brigade, Dutton, on the skirmish line with his men, was mortally wounded. He was evacuated from the field and taken to a hospital ship in Baltimore Harbor, where he died in his 26th year on June 5. He received the brigadier star while on his deathbed.

After Col. Arthur H. Dutton's death, he was buried with full military honors at Arlington National Cemetery in Virginia. Maj. Hiram Crosby, who took command of the Connecticut 21st after Dutton and Lieutenant Colonel Burpee died, had this to say of Dutton in his report to the Connecticut adjutant general Morse: "Bold and chivalrous, with a nice sense of honor, a judgment quick and decisive, an unwavering zeal for his chosen profession, he was, in every respect, a thorough soldier. As an engineer, his talents were of the highest order, and at the time of his death, he had attained the rank of Captain of Engineers in the regular army. By his companions in arms, he will never be forgotten, and to them, his last resting place will be as a shrine commemorating the friendships which not the rude shock of war, or the lapse of time, can blight or destroy." Arthur H. Dutton Post No. 36 raised money beginning in 1885 for the creation of a monument honoring the men who fought in the Civil War. In 1902, the Soldiers Monument was erected, and Dutton Park in Wallingford, seen here, was named in Colonel Dutton's honor.

Dr. Benjamin Franklin Harrison was born in 1811. After graduating from Yale College, he established a medical practice in 1836 treating the bumps, bruises, and various ailments of Wallingford citizens. He married Susan Lewis, daughter of Frederick Lewis and Sina Hall, in 1837. When Susan died two years later, leaving him with an infant daughter, Dr. Harrison threw himself into his work. He moved to Paris to further his study of medicine, and upon his return, he brought the latest in medical treatments to his Wallingford patients. Dr. Harrison served as a surgeon in the Civil War, where poor water quality and sanitation were responsible for illness and death. This experience compelled him to lobby for a town water works service, becoming the town's first chairman of the Water Commission in 1885. He also kept a daily record of weather conditions from his house on Main Street, measuring wind speeds and temperatures from 1856 until his death in 1886. The records of Dr. B.F. Harrison's meteorological data are currently held within the Yale University archives. (Courtesy of the Wallingford Historical Society.)

Dr. Harrison was an early educator and helped define the educational practices within Wallingford's school system. He was admired for his intelligence, kindness, and great humor. His third wife and widow, Sarah, donated land and dedicated a park in memory of her late husband. In 1919, twenty-seven red oak trees were planted in Harrison Park (above) to honor the fallen soldiers of World War I. The oak tree at the entrance was planted in memory of Dr. Harrison. The first dedication ceremony was held on May 30, 1919. At right, Sina Hall Lewis, mother of Dr. Harrison's first wife, Susan, sits for a portrait after the Civil War. She helped raise her granddaughter when Dr. Harrison left for Europe shortly after his wife's death. (Above, courtesy of the Wallingford Public Library; right, courtesy of the Wallingford Historical Society.)

Two of the most notable families in Wallingford during the 1800s were the Simpson and Tibbits families. Pictured above at center is Elizabeth Simpson Hull, the matriarch of the Simpson family. She was the daughter of Wallingford industrialist Samuel Simpson. When he died in 1894, Elizabeth inherited his stately home on North Main Street. To the right of her is Elizabeth Hull's daughter Georgiana Hull Tibbits. Crouching at right is Charles Tibbits, husband to Georgiana. The family accumulated their vast wealth from the silver manufacturing industry. Below is the large Victorian mansion built in 1891 for Georgiana and Charles Tibbits as a wedding gift from Georgiana's father, Gurdon Hull. The Simpson and Tibbits families were known for their garden parties and charitable works and were highly regarded within the Wallingford community. The local society pages followed these important families, much like the celebrities of today, regularly reporting on even the most mundane activities in their lives. (Both, courtesy of Robert A. Taber.)

By the end of the 19th century, the success of the silver industry was advancing Wallingford in new directions. Some of the distinguished families began displaying their wealth in a manner not previously seen in the town. Above, Margaret Tibbits Tabor, great-granddaughter of prosperous Samuel Simpson, is seen being driven through Wallingford by the family footman. At right, Georgiana Hull Tibbits is dressed in all her finery around 1894. At the end of the 19th century, as sidewalks were installed and streets were improved, it was not uncommon to see the ladies of Wallingford strolling Main Street in hoop skirts and elaborate hats on their way to church. (Above, courtesy of Robert A. Taber; right, courtesy of the Wallingford Public Library.)

Jared Potter Whittlesey was born in Wallingford in 1787 and was descended from the old colonial Whittlesey family. He served in the War of 1812 and later became a wholesale flour merchant in New York City. He moved back to Wallingford where he and his wife, Lydia Archer Whittlesey (below), built a large mansion and raised 10 children. In addition, he was a successful farmer and had extensive flour mills in New York State. Whittlesey was also known for his philanthropy and devotion to the betterment and beautification of Wallingford. He helped organize the Ornamental Tree Society in 1846 with his sons and planted elm trees throughout Wallingford. His charitable work included the Children's Aid Society and the Association to Improve the Conditions of the Poor, and he gave extensively to various churches in town. His wife, Lydia, tragically died in 1869 after her skirts caught on fire, and Jared Potter Whittlesey died one month later.

The Wallingford Trotting and Cycling Association (later known as the Wallingford Driving and Cycling Association) operated from 1892 until 1910 and provided a variety of entertainment for Victorian Wallingford. The racetrack was on the north side of East Center Street, just east of East Main Street. Records note that the grandstand and fencing cost $250 when it was installed in 1895. The starting bell is currently housed at the Wallingford Historical Society. (Courtesy of the Wallingford Historical Society.)

The Wallingford National Band was founded in 1870. One of its notable members was William P. (Tony) Smith, born in Middlefield in 1837. He worked as a farmer before enlisting in Boston with Company F of the 54th Massachusetts Regiment. After the war, Smith came to Wallingford, was given land near the Quinnipiac River, and earned his living as a hunter and trapper until his passing in 1916. Smith, an excellent drummer and fifer, joined the Wallingford National Band, which was founded shortly after the Civil War and was active through the 1890s. In addition to playing in parades and fife and drum corps events, the band served with the 2nd Company Governor's Foot Guard. Smith also founded the Dred Not Fife and Drum Corps, the first African American drum corps in Connecticut, and was also responsible for the first drum corps convention in Connecticut.

On August 9, 1878, a "whirlwind" formed above Wallingford's Community Lake and headed toward Main Street, leaving a path of destruction and debris all the way to Durham. A whirlwind, or tornado, was a rare occurrence in New England, but regardless, the results were devastating. Thirty-four people were killed and 70 injured, and over 30 houses and 50 barns were destroyed. Most Holy Trinity Church and the North Main Street School, gifted by Moses Yale Beach, were left in ruins. Immediately following the storm, which was estimated to last only 90 seconds, the town bell rang, prompting citizens to rush to the aid of the survivors. Farmers from the east side of town, alarmed by debris in their fields, raced to the village to assist. The entire community went into action, tending to the dead and injured and forming committees to raise aid and provisions for the survivors. At least 25 families were left completely destitute. By the next morning, thousands of gawkers arrived on foot, wagon, and train to view the disaster, prompting town warden C.D. Yale to dispatch the militia to control the crowds and protect the property of the victims. At the time, Connecticut meteorological scientists employed Dr. B.F. Harrison's instruments and theories in order to understand the phenomenon. The tornado, estimated to be an F4, is considered one of the deadliest in Connecticut history. (Courtesy of the New York Public Library digital collections.)

John P. Stevenson and Company was a popular men's clothing store in Wallingford in the late 1800s. Stevenson came to Wallingford in 1853 and established his clothing business first in the William Wallace Block and later in the Simpson Block on Main Street. It was described by Charles Bancroft Gillespie in *Souvenir History of Wallingford, Connecticut* as "the finest and best patronized of Wallingford clothing houses." This advertisement appeared on a trade card, a popular form of advertising and a collectible item in the 19th century. It was designed and printed by M.F. Tobin Litho, one of the largest publishing houses in New York City.

Wallingford's first post office was located on Simpson Court in 1798, and James Carrington was its first postmaster until 1820. In the 1820s, mail service was only twice a week. The post office was moved to multiple locations in town throughout the 19th century and finally found a home in the Simpson Block in 1887. At the time, it had over 600 lock boxes and 300 call boxes, with six mailings per day. Some of Wallingford's colonial descendants held the position of postmaster, including William Elton, Samuel Cook, Samuel Dutton, Jerome B. Pomeroy, Lorenzo Lewis, and D.W. Ives. A new post office, pictured here, opened in 1913 on the corner of Main and Center Streets. The building was torn down 60 years later to construct Wallingford's present-day post office.

Charles Dwight Yale II, born in 1810, was the son of Charles Yale I, a pioneer in the manufacturing of Britannia ware in Wallingford, and a fourth great-grandson of Wallingford founder Thomas Yale. When C.D. Yale was 16 years old, he was sent to Richmond, Virginia, to manage the family's store, selling Wallingford-manufactured Japanned-ware, tinware, and Britannia ware, eventually building the largest warehouse in that city. He became a leader and peacemaker during the post–Civil War reconstruction, helping to bring Virginia back into the Union. Yale returned to Wallingford after the war and became the treasurer of Simpson, Hall, Miller & Company, one of the first companies that merged to become the International Silver Company. C.D. Yale, much beloved in Wallingford, was considered a gifted speaker and a gentleman of strong character.

Three

WORSHIPING

The Puritans who settled Wallingford subscribed to strict religious beliefs. They were passionate about their religious freedom, and worshiping was at the center of community life. Wallingford's first tax (1673) was imposed in order to fund the ministry. In 1675, the First Church Society was started by order of a town meeting, and Samuel Street was installed as the church's first pastor. His residence was built by the townspeople, and it still stands today at 238 South Main Street. He remained pastor for 42 years. Samuel Street was the great-grandfather of Wallingford's Lyman Hall. Today, Wallingford can give thanks to its Puritan ancestors, whose quest for independence and the freedom to practice their religion as they saw fit gave rise to the self-reliance, frugality, industriousness, and perseverance that became the cornerstones of the community and enabled Wallingford to thrive.

The First Church Society is today's First Congregational Church, located at the southwest corner of Center and Main Streets. It was originally a simple meetinghouse on the east side of today's Simpson Court, and prior to that, the townspeople met in the homes of Lt. Nathanial Merriman or Samuel Munson to hear John Harriman, a layman, preach on the Sabbath. No matter where the services took place in Wallingford's early history, attendance at the all-day service on the Sabbath was mandatory.

Worshiping God in Puritan Wallingford was a strict affair. Sabbath services started early in the morning and lasted all day. Meetinghouses were cold and drafty, the parishioners' behavior was monitored, and punishment was meted out for mischievous childish antics, sleeping during services, and general disruptiveness. To mitigate the interminable lengthy sermons and the uncomfortable conditions, Sabbath houses were built around the meetinghouse. Unlike the meetinghouse, Sabbath houses were allowed to have chimneys and offered a respite for parishioners to take their midday meal along with a bit of warmth before returning to the meetinghouse for additional services. The unrelenting daily toil needed to sustain the basics of life and the long hours of worship brings to mind H.L. Mencken's famous remark that a Puritan is one who suspects "somewhere someone is having a good time." And woe betide anyone in Wallingford who did not conform to the strictures of Puritan life. Wallingford's own late-17th-century Benham witch trials attest to the beliefs in supernatural powers and that both the clergy and townsfolk feared the devil was ready to pounce on anyone who was not the purest of heart and most pious in worship.

The strict control of the church over daily life began to crack as the young town and the country at large became home to a growing population. In 1708, the Act of Toleration allowed religious sects to worship separately. A revolution was on the horizon. Wallingford's tight-knit religious community had thrived under the leadership of Pastor Street and his successor Pastor

Whittlesey, but when young Reverend Dana came to town, sparks started to fly. This dissention among the parishioners ran deep and was referred to as the Dana Controversy or the Wallingford Controversy. It resulted in a separation of worship and ultimately affected the future of religious practice in Wallingford. Roughly one-third of the First Church Society members, many of whom were prominent townspeople, left the First Church Society to become members of the Wells Society. They worshiped in a humble building on the current site of St. Paul's Episcopal Church.

Before the mid-century mark, Wallingford was home to the Episcopalian and the Baptist sects. The Episcopalian church began as early as 1741 with a congregation of families from Wallingford, Cheshire, and North Haven. Their original house of worship was in the area of Pond Hill, and was called Union Church. Over time, the church became known as St. Paul's Episcopal Church, and the congregation built its first structure on Christian Street (1757), where the first organ in Wallingford was installed. Most of the church members were loyal to the crown, and political divisiveness rumbled from the pulpit throughout the town. Since 1868, St. Paul's gothic-inspired, brownstone Episcopalian church has stood at its current location on North Main Street. The Episcopal congregation expanded to Yalesville in 1868 when St. John the Evangelist Episcopal Church was established.

The First Baptist Church of Wallingford was initially part of a congregation in Meriden and dates to 1735. It was not until decades later that the church was recognized in Wallingford. The gift of a church bell was received from England's Lord Wallingford in 1817, and by 1821, a meetinghouse had been erected on the site of the current church. The steeple was added and the building enlarged in the late 1840s. A fire on December 4, 1869, destroyed the building. The following day at a service held in the new town hall, $10,000 was pledged for a new building, a significant amount of money given the small number of attendees. Just over a year later, on December 29, 1870, the new church was dedicated. At the time, the cost of construction was $30,000, with an additional $6,200 for an organ, bell, and furnishings.

The Catholics came to Wallingford in the mid-19th century and held their first Mass in a private home at the corner of North Main and High Streets in 1847. Ten years later, they had raised enough money to build Most Holy Trinity Church on North Colony Street at the corner of Parker Street. Two decades later, the church was destroyed during the Wallingford Disaster of 1878. The church was rebuilt on its current site and dedicated on Thanksgiving Day, November 24, 1887. In addition to Most Holy Trinity Church, today's Catholic community in Wallingford includes parishioners of Our Lady of Fatima, Church of the Resurrection, and SS. Peter and Paul Roman Catholic Church.

The Yalesville Methodist congregation was formed in 1867. They shared their religious home with the local Baptists until, within a year, a large donation by local businessman and factory owner Charles Parker enabled them to purchase the building for themselves. The present church on Church Street was erected in 1899.

The exploration of religious freedom in Wallingford was not limited to traditional Protestant or Catholic sects. John Humphrey Noyes came to Wallingford in the mid-19th century to open a satellite community of his Oneida, New York, community. Known as the Wallingford Community, it was established on 240 acres near the current site of the Masonic Home. The Oneida community of Wallingford fostered a printing company, the production of flatware, silk thread, agricultural products, and other industries. They dammed the Quinnipiac River for waterpower and created Community Lake. This industrious community held unconventional beliefs about the resurrection of Christ, marriage, procreation, and child rearing. The community disbanded by 1880, with members either returning to the original site in Oneida, New York, or emigrating to Canada.

Typical colonial thriftiness is depicted in the simple architecture of the meetinghouse. The Pond Hill meetinghouse was home to the Union Church parish, formed in 1741 by Church of England parishioners from Wallingford and North Haven. The first church meetinghouse was constructed of rough-hewn logs. Men sat along one side of an interior wall and women sat opposite. It was the religious, civic, and social center of the town. The Wells Society began services in its meetinghouse in 1762. Although the society dissolved in 1787, its sturdy meetinghouse prevailed for 80 years.

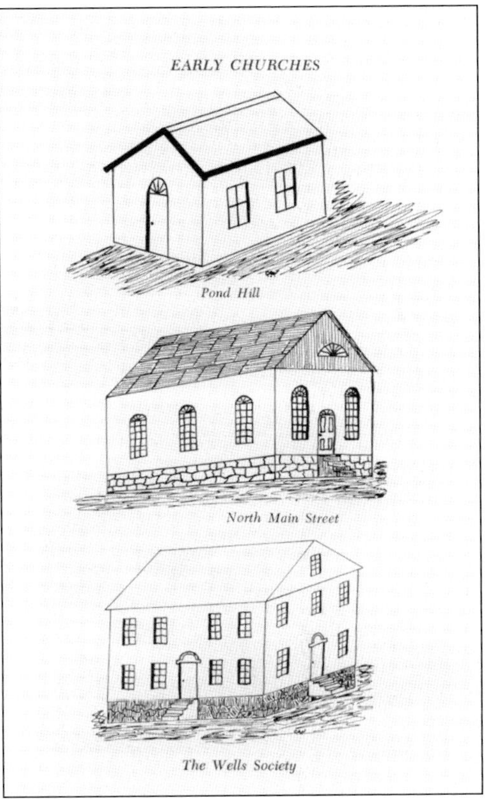

Reverend Street led the colonists in prayer, guided their religious life, and influenced civic affairs for 42 years. His sure-footed legacy of traditional preaching was continued by his successor, Reverend Whittlesey. Rev. James Dana was just 23 years old and a recent Harvard graduate when he was installed as pastor. Dana's doctrine and manner were immediately called into question. He would further alienate a portion of the congregation, resulting in a split of New Lights versus Old Lights and the birth of the Wells Society.

Pastors.

REV. SAMUEL STREET.

Called in 1672. Under his supervision the church was organized. He died January 16, 1717, aged 82 years.

REV. SAMUEL WHITTLESEY.

Ordained colleague pastor with Mr. Street, May, 1710. He died April 25, 1752, aged 67 years.

REV. JAMES DANA, D. D.

Ordained October 12, 1758. He removed to New Haven in 1789, where he became pastor of the First Church. He died August, 1812, aged 77 years.

REV. JAMES NOYES.

Ordained colleague pastor with Dr. Dana, May 4, 1785. His pastoral relation was dissolved June 5, 1832, and he died February 18, 1844, aged 79 years.

REV. EDWIN R. GILBERT.

Ordained October 3, 1832.

Confession of Faith.

ART. I. We, as a church, believe that Jehovah, the true and eternal God, who made, supports, and governs the world, is perfect in natural and moral excellence, and that he exists in three persons, the Father, the Son, and the Holy Ghost, who possess the same nature, and are equal in every divine perfection.

ART. II. We believe that the Scriptures of the Old and New Testament were written by holy men, as they were moved by the Holy Ghost, and are the only infallible rule of doctrine and duty.

ART. III. We believe that God has made all things for himself; that known unto him are all his works from the beginning, and that he governs all things according to the counsel of his own will.

ART. IV. We believe that men are immortal and accountable; that the law of God is perfect, and his government just and good; and that all rational beings are bound to approve, love, and obey them.

ART. V. We believe that in consequence of the apostacy of Adam, sin and misery have been introduced into the world, and that all men, unless renewed by the Holy Spirit, are destitute of holiness, and are under the curse of the divine law.

Born in England in 1635, Rev. Samuel Street was one of Wallingford's founding fathers. After teaching Latin at Hopkins Grammar School in New Haven, Street was removed to Wallingford in 1673 and became the first pastor of the village. In 1673, a town meeting was held, and it was decided that a house should be raised on a six-acre plot in the village for Reverend Street at the town's expense. In addition, he was granted another 200 acres of land and became a profitable farmer. It was common practice for the early town leaders to lure ministers to Wallingford with the promise of a house and land. (His successor, Rev. Samuel Whittlesey, was also promised a house; however, it was stipulated that he was required to provide his own nails and glass for the project.) Reverend Street was the great-grandfather of the Hall brothers, Lyman, Street, and Giles, each of whom played an active role in Wallingford's Revolutionary War era. The Rev. Samuel Street house stands today at 238 South Main Street (Courtesy of William Burgess.)

Edwin Randolph Gilbert (right), son of Peyton R. and Anna Gilbert of Hebron, Connecticut, was born on February 10, 1808. His father was a highly regarded and prosperous farmer who served as a representative in the legislature and the state senate. Reverend Gilbert graduated from Yale College in 1829. Like his father, he too was held in high regard by his fellow students and teachers. Following graduation, he enrolled in the theological department at Yale and finished his course of study a year later. He followed Rev. James Noyes as the fifth pastor of the First Church Society in Wallingford. Reverend Gilbert's wife, Dorcas Dutton Gilbert, is pictured below. (Both, courtesy of the Wallingford Historical Society.)

The First Congregational Church can trace its roots to the town's inception. It was then, and still is now, at the center of town. The cornerstone of the brick edifice at the corner of Center and Main Streets was laid in 1869.

St. Paul's Episcopal Church has a fascinating history that reflects significant events over the past three centuries. As a member of the Church of England, its leadership and congregation were suspect during the Revolutionary War. When fire destroyed the church in 1867, Samuel Simpson and E. Hinsdale Ives agreed to contribute to rebuilding. They were able to convince Moses Beach to donate as well by pointing out the church would be in view directly opposite his residence.

Although the beginnings of Wallingford's First Baptist Church date to 1735, it was not recognized until 1817, when it established itself in the center of town. During this time, the gift of a church bell was received from England's Lord Wallingford. A fire destroyed the original building in 1869, and the current brick building was built in the Romanesque Revival style in 1870. Its spire and beautiful round stained-glass window have become landmarks in town. (Courtesy of William Burgess.)

This view of the south side of the Church of the Most Holy Trinity dates to 1925; note the men working on the building. The design was based on the parish church of Cougher, Ireland, home of Father Mallon. The beloved pastor began his 30-year service in 1867.

These two Catholic parishes were organized to serve the growing Catholic population on the west and east sides of town, respectively. Our Lady of Fatima (Yalesville) was built on land donated by T. Joseph and Mary Esther McNally. It opened its doors for services in 1956. The contemporary architecture of the Church of the Resurrection makes it unique. Contractors Buckingham Routh of New Haven built the church in 1965. Elements from nature decorate the interior of the church, including a phoenix in front of the altar, butterflies carved on the sides of the altar, pelicans adorning the tabernacle, a sunburst hanging above the tabernacle, and a dove on the front of the pulpit. (Both, courtesy of William Burgess.)

Polish immigrants bought land on North Orchard Street and established SS. Peter and Paul Parish in 1924. The mission-style church was designed by architect Henry F. Ludorf of Hartford. Its first Mass was held in May of the following year. Its beautiful and elaborate interior has welcomed the surrounding community ever since.

Born in Meriden to Konstanty and Eva Nowakowski, Ladislaus Nowakowski attended St. Stanislaus and St. Rose Parochial Schools in Meriden and studied for the priesthood at St. Thomas Seminary in Bloomfield as well as at SS. Cyril and Methodius Seminary in Orchard Lake, Michigan, and St. Bernard's Seminary in New York. He was ordained on March 20, 1920, by Bishop John J. Nilan at St. Joseph's Cathedral, Hartford. Father Nowakowski was pastor of SS. Peter and Paul Parish from 1927 to 1944, where he was nicknamed "Father Sunshine."

The beautiful and colorful stained-glass windows and redbrick facade of the Yalesville Methodist Church face Church Street in Yalesville. Its presence has been a constant since the late 19th century. An addition for a church school was added in 1957. (Courtesy of William Burgess.)

Founded in 1891, Zion Lutheran Church found its first home in 1911 on the corner of Ward Street and South Whittlesey Avenue. In search of a larger space, the church relocated to Pond Hill Road when a six-acre turkey farm became available for purchase. The new church was built in 1977 and added a preschool in 1986. The expansive property has been home to numerous church picnics and outdoor services in the summertime.

Heritage Baptist Church describes itself as an "Independent Fundamental Bible Believing Baptist Church." It was established in 1978 and held its first services in Yalesville. The church moved to the former Whittlesey Avenue School in 1982 and purchased the building in 1988. (Courtesy of William Burgess.)

Calvary United Pentecostal Church has services on Sundays and on Wednesday evenings. Many of the sermons are available through the church's website. In addition to the general congregation, it ministers to children, teens, and women and supports select projects for missionaries around the globe. (Courtesy of William Burgess.)

For over 100 years, Beth Israel Synagogue has been the center of Wallingford's Jewish community. Located on North Orchard Street, the synagogue has expanded since its 1908 inception and continues to maintain its vibrancy and commitment to the congregation and the community at large. (Courtesy of William Burgess.)

The Islamic Center of Wallingford found a home in the former Ward Street Church of Christ building on South Whittlesey Avenue. After remodeling and renovating the space, the mosque opened its doors in January 2019. (Courtesy of William Burgess.)

Four

LEARNING

Education in 17th-century Wallingford was influenced by the Puritans' strong religious beliefs, and Bible reading and studying sermons were essential elements of early colonial life. The importance of education was recognized in 1650 by the General Court in Hartford and served as the first step in directing parents to ensure their children could read and comprehend the laws they were expected to live by. Two principles were set forth by this early court and remain the basis for Connecticut's educational system today. The first is that the state should compel parents and legal guardians to educate their children. The second is that public money, raised by taxes, could be used to pay for education. These stipulations gave the Puritan community of Wallingford a framework for educating its citizenry.

At its inception, Wallingford was home to about 50 children, and their parents were responsible for educating them. In 1678, a motion was passed to hire a schoolmaster, resulting in Wallingford's first education tax (1679). Payment was to be made in quantities of wheat and corn, levied according to income. Ensign Munson was hired; however, his tenure lasted only a few months. Eliasaph Preston then took over, and various other schoolmasters followed for only short intervals at a time. Without a schoolhouse, students were educated in private homes, and it was not until 1702 that a modest 20-square-foot schoolhouse was erected near the town center. When Henry Bates was hired as schoolmaster in 1711, Wallingford education found some permanence. Bates remained the town's schoolmaster for at least a decade. The community had great respect for him and honored him with a seat in the first pew of the meetinghouse gallery. During this time, the education curriculum focused on reading, writing, mathematics, poems, and prayers. In 1724, a larger one-story schoolhouse was built on South Main Street across from the current site of the Wallingford Historical Society. In addition, a one-room schoolhouse for Yalesville was built on the east side of the Quinnipiac River, north of the present-day entrance to Route 15, located on Route 5. The South Main Street School was replaced in 1824 with a new two-room, two-story building, which operated until 1913. The Yalesville School was relocated in 1800 close to the site where the newly named Mary Fritz Elementary School now sits.

Wallingford's sprawling growth required schoolhouses to serve children living outside of the town center, and the "farm district schools" were established. Between 1811 and the late 1860s, multiple farm district schoolhouses existed to serve the educational needs of youths living with their families on farms and agricultural lands throughout the community.

The 19th century brought new challenges to Wallingford's commitment to education. Compulsory education was debated, and education taxes were controversial. In 1868, Connecticut passed the Free School Law, eliminating tuition at public schools and transferring the fiscal burden to taxpayers. The law made each town responsible for raising enough money to operate its schools for a minimum of six months per year. In 1885, a bill passed compelling children to "regularly" attend school from ages 9 through 16; however, it excluded children considered destitute of suitable clothing. Possibly these laws were in response to the combination of the labor needs for the industrial revolution and the waves of immigrants arriving from southern and eastern Europe. By the mid-19th century, 11 schools were serving the Wallingford community. Generous donations by local businessmen Moses Yale Beach in 1868 and Samuel Simpson in 1884 gave the town land for the express purpose of education. The Moses Y. Beach property consisted of three acres at the corner of North Main and Christian Streets, where the North Main Street School was built in 1871. The four-story Mansard-roofed structure was infamously damaged by the tornado known as the Wallingford Disaster of 1878. Today, this property is the current site of Moses Y. Beach Elementary School. The Simpson school built in 1884 was near the Simpson, Hall, Miller & Company on East Center Street, where today a condominium and townhouse complex stand. Other elementary schools included the Cottage School (1868), Colony Street School (1881), Whittlesey Avenue School (1896), and the Washington Street School (c. 1896).

The 20th and 21st centuries continued to bring changes to education and are reflected in the area's schools today: eight elementary schools—Cook Hill, E.C. Stevens, Highland, and Moses Y. Beach (pre-kindergarten to second grade) and Parker Farms, Pond Hill, Mary G. Fritz (formerly Yalesville), and Rock Hill (covering grades three to five); two middle schools—Dag Hammarskjold and James H. Moran; and two high schools—Lyman Hall and Mark T. Sheehan. These institutions, under the leadership of the Wallingford Board of Education and superintendent of schools, serve to educate today's population of 5,675 students. The town's ongoing commitment to education continues to enable Wallingford students to meet the challenging and changing needs of the community and the world at large. In addition to educating children, today's Wallingford Adult Education offers residents 18 years and older a variety of classes and activities, including completing a high school education, strengthening English language skills, exploring new interests, or preparing for a new career path.

Private education has a long history in Wallingford. There were many private schools over the past 350 years, including a coeducational traditional school started in 1794 by George Washington Stanley; a school for young ladies operated by Hannah Hall and her daughter Ruth Hall Hart in 1795; the Union Academy (1809–1833); the Gothic School for Manners operated by Sarah F. Carrington in the mid-19th century; Rosemary Hall and the Choate School for Boys, both established in the late 19th century and later combined to become the current Choate Rosemary Hall preparatory coed school; the Phelps School for Girls (1900–1916); Holy Trinity School (1913 to present); the Putnam School (1917–1951); and Heritage Baptist Academy (1982 to present).

Moses Yale Beach (right) married Nancy Day (below) in 1819, and they had five children. The two later divorced, and Moses Beach went on to marry Julia Ann Kelly, with whom he had two children. Beach sponsored many causes in Wallingford, the most famous being his donation of $10,000 and the land to build a new school at the corner of Christian and North Main Streets, the site of the present-day Moses Y. Beach Elementary School. He was a great proponent of public education and would offer prizes to children who excelled academically. On one occasion, over 600 Wallingford schoolchildren marched to his residence where they saluted him with cheers and then proceeded to an awards ceremony where Beach was the main benefactor of over $500 in prize money.

Martha De Ette Simpson (known as De Ette) was born in Wallingford to Samuel and Martha De Etta Benham Simpson in 1841. She was an original member of the Ladies Library and Reading Room, which was founded in 1881. It was a subscription library with members paying dues to have the privilege of borrowing books. Without a permanent home, the Ladies Library met in rented rooms in both the Wallace Block and Simpson Block in the center of town. De Ette predeceased her father, Samuel, passing at the age of 41. On his deathbed, her father, Samuel, made a lasting testament to his daughter by donating the land at 60 North Main Street and the funds to build ($25,000) and sustain ($20,000) a library in his daughter's memory. A plaque inside the front double doors of the building commemorates Simpson's donation and honors the inspiration De Ette Simpson provided for this generous gift to the community.

The original library building (above) at 60 North Main Street was designed by Wilson Potter. The cornerstone was laid on September 21, 1899, by Margaret Tibbits, Samuel Simpson's great-granddaughter. That same year, it became a free library. In 1958, membership was opened to men as well as women, and the name was legally changed to the Wallingford Public Library. Today, the building is home to the Library Wine Bar and Bistro. Pictured at right is Marie Gannon gazing at a display of taxidermic birds in the children's section of the original library. In the 19th and early 20th centuries, taxidermy was very popular and displayed in public spaces as well as private homes.

Daniel R. Knight graduated from Amherst College in 1891. State education records show he was working as principal of North Main Street School and also as superintendent of Wallingford schools during the time immediately following his graduation through 1897 and maybe longer.

The North Main Street School is shown here around the late 1880s. Originally, the school had four floors with the high school students being taught on the upper floors. This photograph shows the school after it had been modified and rebuilt following the damage of the 1878 tornado.

Marion L. Preston was the music teacher at North Main Street School in the latter 19th century. Music education as an area of study for public school students originated in Boston in 1838 with singing teacher Lowell Mason. Students were taught "by rote and by note," and music education became a popular area of study.

In 1950–1951, the North Main Street School was razed and replaced with Moses Y. Beach Elementary School. Before the demolition, construction began on the new elementary school's foundation. Note the partial view of the house at left built by the C.F. Wooding Company in 1923 and still standing today.

A part of District 4 in 1868, the North Farms School was in the northeast section of town. As a typical farm district school, the one-room schoolhouse was attended by approximately 40 students of various ages who were taught by a single teacher.

Arbor Day was celebrated at public schools nationally, and North Farms School was no exception. It was regarded as an opportunity for children to observe and appreciate the natural world. This c. 1902 Arbor Day celebration would have included songs, recitations, and the planting of trees and shrubs around the schoolhouse.

Playgrounds were initiated during the Progressive Movement of the late 19th century and the early 20th century, and Wallingford's Margaret Taber was a champion of introducing playgrounds to the town. Here, the Washington Street School playground is dominated by male students under the supervision of their teacher. Note the boy in the white shirt attempting to pole vault.

Claire Banks succeeded Lula Bartholomew as a kindergarten teacher at Colony Street School in 1901. The Colony Street School has a tumultuous history, being used as a morgue following the tornado of 1878 and then damaged by fire in 1900. The school closed its doors in 1949, only to reopen for a year while the Moses Y. Beach School was being built in 1951.

Wallingford-born and a signer of the Declaration of Independence, Lyman Hall is honored as the namesake of Lyman Hall High School. When the school was first built in 1916 on South Main Street, there was considerable debate about the name. Moses Y. Beach, the 19th-century philanthropist, was a top contender, as was Wallingford High School.

The Lyman Hall High School band is shown in front of the high school on South Main Street, the site of the current town hall. Dr. Richard Otto appears at lower right. Dr. Otto led the Lyman Hall music program for 37 years.

In 1961, Dag Hammarskjold, the second secretary general of the United Nations, was killed in a plane crash about the same time the new middle school on Pond Hill Road was nearing completion. The new school was named in his honor, but not without controversy. It was the first time a school had been named after a non-Wallingford resident. (Courtesy of William Burgess.)

The Mark T. Sheehan High School on the west side of town was built in 1971 on land that had been part of the McNally Farm. The school's namesake is Dr. Sheehan, a local doctor who practiced medicine for over 50 years and was the Wallingford health officer for decades.

This postcard image of the Atwater House on the Choate campus shows the center of the Rosemary Hall School for girls. The school's founder, Mary Atwater Choate, was a descendent of Wallingford's captain Caleb Atwater, famous for hosting Gen. George Washington at his home and supporting the Revolutionary War.

An elaborate daisy chain decorates the May pole and is the focal point of these Rosemary Hall graduates on prize day in 1905. The Atwater House can be seen in the background. Rosemary Hall was founded on the grounds of Mary Atwater Choate's ancestral land, Rosemary Farm. (Courtesy of Choate Rosemary Hall archives.)

Standing on the lawn of the Wallingford Rosemary Hall campus around 1900, these four schoolmates appear to be good friends. From left to right are Ethyl Clinton, Marion Oliver, Grace Douglas, and Evelyn Movius. (Courtesy of Choate Rosemary Hall archives.)

The Curtis House, just south of the corner of Christian and North Elm Streets on the Choate campus, was built around an existing house in 1850 by Roderic Curtis and is known as an envelope house. From 1908 through the mid-1990s, it was the residence of Choate headmasters. In 2002, it was renamed the Sally Hart Lodge and Alumni Center and accommodates visitors to campus.

The Seymour St. John Chapel on the Choate campus honors the Episcopal priest headmaster who saw the chapel as "a rallying place for the best that is in boys and men" and believed spiritual guidance was essential to a well-rounded education. Seymour St. John was Choate headmaster for 40 years.

A Choate class photograph shows John F. Kennedy sitting second from left in the first row. Kennedy and his brother Joe attended Choate in the early 1930s. While Joe excelled in sports and academics, his younger brother was a prankster and nicknamed himself and his friends "The Choate Muckers Club."

Students at the Phelps School for Young Ladies are pictured in front of the school at Academy and North Main Streets in the early 1900s. The girls are dressed in costumes. Margaret Tibbetts, first row, third from right, is dressed as a baker. Tibbets was Samuel Simpson's great-granddaughter and later married Herschel Taber.

The Phelps School for Young Ladies moved to the Judd Mansion on South Main Street from its former home at the corner of Academy and North Main Streets. Here, the students are on the lawn in front of the former mansion's carriage house around 1910. The carriage house stands today at its original location.

Commemorating milestones in students' academic and religious education at Holy Trinity School was cause for celebration. Assembled on the school's front steps around the 1920s, these students are adorned with ribbons and flowers. Although the school has expanded and gone through many renovations, some of its original architectural elements are still intact today.

Founded in 1913, Holy Trinity School focuses on building a faith community as well as academics for students in kindergarten through eighth grade. Fr. John Carroll and the Sisters of Mercy were the original leaders of the school. It is on the corner of Center Street and North Whittlesey Avenue.

Five

Farming

Wallingford's founding fathers were charged with creating a plantation from sandy plains, rocky terrain, and dense forests. It became the work of the entire village to cultivate the treasured seeds they had bartered for or brought with them to this new land. Crops of Indian corn and flax, potatoes and turnips, and hay and rye were coaxed from the rocky reddish-brown soil. Vegetables, meat, and poultry gave sustenance, and flax and wool provided clothing and bedding. The relentless hard work required to grow vegetables and grain, raise livestock, and build the necessary tools, barns, and fences was a communal affair. Farmers helped farmers. The survival of the plantation was the responsibility of each man, woman, and child. The oxen plowed fields and the hand-tilled kitchen gardens exemplified the determination and fortitude necessary to lay a foundation for the future farming community.

Learning how to cultivate and manage the land was an ongoing process, and Wallingford's colonial farming practices evolved from Native American and English traditions. Initially livestock roamed freely, and the early barns in the community were used to house grain and hay. The free-range animals needed to be identified, and the farmers used creative ways to brand their cattle. Sam Cooke used "a half penny under each ear and a half crop on the underside of the right ear" to mark his animals. To protect crops and gardens from being overrun, fencing became a priority and official fence watchers were appointed.

The colonists' hard work started to pay off, and gradually, the sustenance farming culture began to change. Orchards were producing a wide variety of fruit, and fields of broom corn were harvested for the production and exportation of brooms. Agriculture was becoming a scientific endeavor, and by the late 1800s, there were more than 200 working farms in Wallingford. As Wallingford's farms expanded and became more established, transportation improved as well, and farmers were able to shift to a commercial economy.

Wallingford's agricultural community continued to thrive in the 20th century. More efficient farming practices allowed for larger farms and specialization of products. The Hall Brothers Hatchery, located on Cook Hill Road, was producing and shipping 16 million baby chicks per year in 1945. Wallingford's orchardists and nurserymen were highly regarded for their expertise. Multiple orchards produced fruit and fruit trees for distribution nationally. In 1945, Wallingford had over 70 dairy farms; the largest of these were owned by Beaumont Dairy, Choate School, Gaylord Farms, and the Masonic Home. By the 1960s, the number of dairy farms had decreased to less than 50, and while the number of local farms was dropping, larger farm operations began to acquire the available farmland to substantially grow their cow populations. In the 1970s, Wallingford's dairy industry evolved to the point where it was rivaled only by Ellington as the top "cow town" in the state. Just a decade later, alternatives to dairy farming were becoming more attractive to Wallingford farmers, and by the 1990s, Wallingford farming was on the wane. Land was being repurposed and housing developments and business parks were sprouting up as local farmers sold their land.

Striving to maintain Wallingford's rural charm and balance growth and development, land preservation came to the forefront. Community gardens were established. Local vineyards began producing wine and luring tourists with scenic views. Wallingford instituted a farmland leasing program to preserve land for agricultural use. Today, farming in Wallingford continues to remain vital to the community and can be seen in the continued efforts of local growers and organizations, including Wallingford Grange (1885), Beaumont Farm (1898), Blue Hills Orchard (1904), Geremia Farms (1914), and more recently, Farmer Joe's Gardens and the Community Supported Agriculture (CSA) movement, Wallingford Garden Market (1999), and the Agricultural Science and Technology program at Lyman Hall High School.

Enterprising individuals have capitalized on the current farm-to-table movement, and organic and sustainability concepts in farming and small farming operations are cropping up. The mission of Wallingford's early settlers to provide a sustainable agrarian community was a success. Over the centuries, that agrarian community may have shifted and diminished, but place names and street names still connote the farming history—Parker Farms, North Farms Reservoir, and Farm Hill Drive are but a few of these.

Norman H. Barnes Sr. overlooks his young orchard stock around the 1930s. The Barnes Brothers Nursery Company was begun by noted horticulturist and farmer James Norris Barnes in the late 1890s. The nursery was the most extensive producer of fruit trees and plants in New England. In 1918, in addition to nursery stock, there were 550 acres of farmland and peach orchards. The orchards and nurseries were managed by the Barnes family for three generations. Their operation included peach and apple trees as well as a large quantity of beehives, and it employed a multitude of laborers. Employees, pictured below, are on their way to work the fields of nursery stock on Barnes Road in front of the old Dr. Hull House. According to the January 1908 edition of the *Penn State Farmer*, a publication of Pennsylvania State College's School of Agriculture, "Barnes' orchards are reputed to be the best in New England."

Above, baskets of peaches are ready for market at the Barnes orchards around 1915, and below, a handsome team of horses is ready to take a wagonload of peaches to market. In May 1915, "the prospects for a bumper crop of peaches" in Connecticut was reported in the *Fruit Trade Journal and Produce Record*. In August of that year, the Barnes brothers joined the movement to promote the consumption of peaches through a campaign produced by the Peach Growers Publicity League. With all good intentions, the league planned to attract peach receivers, growers, and shippers interested in advertising peaches to retail buyers.

During the height of the peach harvest season, a dedicated "peach train" ran through central Connecticut on the Airline Railroad, which goes through East Wallingford. The train would be loaded with the crops from Wallingford and area orchards and delivered throughout the state for distribution to regional markets and processing plants such as the Gerber Baby Food plant in Bridgeport, Connecticut. Usually two white flags flew from either side of the engine.

Barnes Brothers Nursery Company workers are getting barrels of apples ready for market in the early 1920s on the east side of the Dr. Hull House at the corner of Barnes Road and North Main Street Extension. Packing the apples using bushel baskets and barrels for shipment was done in the orchard until automation moved the operation into modern apple-packing facilities.

Utilizing whatever type of transportation was available—bicycles, teams of oxen, and flatbed trucks—workers at Barnes Brothers Nursery Company would get out to the fields. Pictured here around 1920, workers are in front of the Barnes's saltbox-style house on Barnes Road, just west of North Main Street Extension. The company's slogan, "Trees Propagated from Bearing Orchards," was a Barnes family hallmark. In addition to fruit trees, the company's 1924 catalog featured hedges and ornamental shrubbery, including roses and peonies. Featured vegetables and fruits raised on the property included cherries, quinces, strawberries, grapes, rhubarb, raspberries, gooseberries, currants, and asparagus.

The blacksmith shop at Blue Hills Orchard was the only building to survive a fire at the orchard, which destroyed all the barns on the east side of School House Road in the early 1920s. The blacksmith, shown above, is carrying his tools and appears to be wearing a pair of chaps to protect his legs from sparks from the horseshoes. The team of mules below is ready to take a load of peaches to market around 1915. Blue Hills Orchard got its start in 1904 when W.A. Henry, former dean of the Agricultural College of Wisconsin, relocated to Wallingford and began growing cabbages. Peaches and cherries followed, and in 1940, Blue Hills Orchard's primary crop became apples. Today, the orchard covers over 300 acres and, in addition to apples, produces peaches, plums, and nectarines.

The hay barn and stable at Rosemary Farm was an integral part of Mary Atwater Choate's childhood. These c. 1897 photographs show an active hay operation. Rosemary Farm had been in Mary Atwater Choate's family for five generations and was her girlhood home. Later, Rosemary Farm became the summer residence for her and her husband, William Gardner Choate, and in 1890, she established Rosemary Hall School for Girls on the property. (Both, courtesy of Choate Rosemary Hall, Huntington-Choate Atwater Scrapbook Collection.)

Rosemary Farm continued its farming operations, providing produce, dairy, and livestock for Rosemary Hall School. The dairy operations and crops were actively farmed around 1897. In 1924, Choate School purchased Choate Farm, and the school dairy was built, providing milk and butter for students and faculty. Choate donated surplus dairy products to the town of Wallingford during the Depression of the 1930s. (Both, courtesy of Choate Rosemary Hall, Huntington-Choate Atwater Scrapbook Collection.)

Rudy Woods (left), of Burlington, is being handed his new Golden Hallcross rooster by Hall Brothers hatchery employee Dana Hartman. Woods also bought Golden Hallcross laying hens at the 222 Cook Hill Road hatchery.

Wallingford's Town Farm was a working farm established to provide the poor, disabled, and elderly residents with shelter and sustenance. It was a working farm that raised produce and livestock. Residents provided the labor, produced home goods, and took care of housekeeping duties. Poor farms were common in Connecticut towns throughout the 19th and early 20th centuries and gradually declined with the passing of the Social Security Act of 1935.

Gaylord Farm Sanatorium was established in 1903 on 250 acres of the Gaylord family farm. Dr. Gaylord sold the acreage to the Anti-Tuberculosis Association at such a reduced price, the association regarded it as a gift and named the sanatorium after him. By 1907, the sanatorium owned 304 acres of pasture and woodland and had 80 acres under cultivation for vegetables and fruits. Additional farm enterprises included a dairy, which provided milk and butter for the patients as well as income from surplus dairy products sold at market. Eggs and poultry were also raised to provide food for sanatorium patients. Gaylord Farms Sanatorium was originally founded to care for tuberculosis patients; with the advent of new drugs to treat the disease, Gaylord expanded its rehabilitation programs. Today, Gaylord Hospital offers wellness programs for patients with chronic pulmonary disorders, stroke, and brain and spinal cord injuries. The Farms Country Club was founded in 1962 on land once owned by Gaylord Farm Sanatorium.

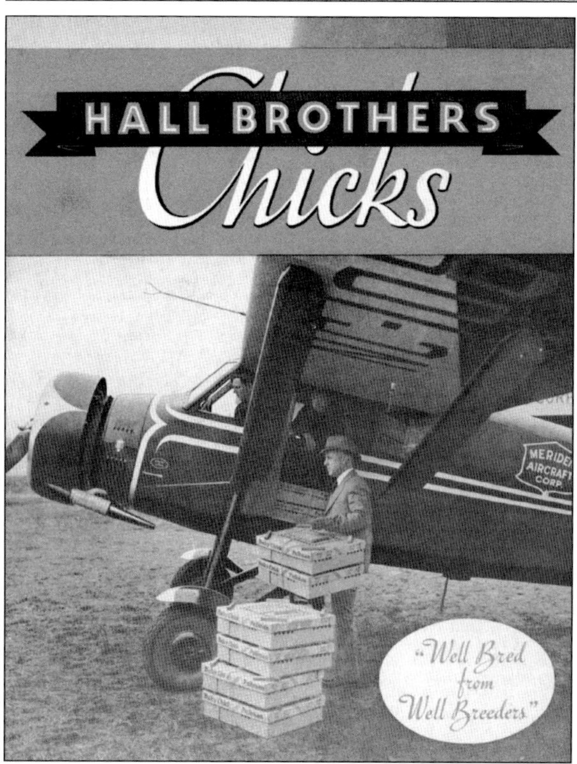

The 1936 photograph of Hall Brothers Hatchery employees above was taken outside the Home Plant Organization in 1936. Located at 222 Cook Hill Road, the Hall Brothers Hatchery was started by Almon B. Hall and his brother Louis in 1911. The advent of electricity revolutionized poultry production, and in 1928, the hatchery junked all its hatching equipment and replaced it with new electric machines capable of a 378,000 egg capacity. The hatchery continued to innovate and grow and by 1939 had an annual hatching capacity of over 1.28 million eggs. Post–World War II growth continued, and the hatchery expanded its operations thanks to growth in distribution provided by the burgeoning airfreight industry, which allowed the hatchery to ship chicks nationwide. As a further testament to the hatchery's prestige, in 1941, members of the congressional Republican Farm Study Committee visited the Hall Brothers Hatchery with their wives, and 16,000 baby chicks were hatched that day.

Pictured above are Richie Masseli and Gordon "Sam" Bentley mixing cement to create the footings for barns on Self's Fieldstone Farm. An early map of Wallingford establishes this farm's origins as 1856. The farm changed hands multiple times before Walter and Bessie Self acquired it in 1913. Bob and Janet Self took over after them. At its peak, Fieldstone Farm annually produced over 1.5 million pounds of milk; farmed about 400 acres; and harvested 400 tons of hay, 100 tons of silage, 2,000 bales of straw, 10 tons of rye seed, and 12 acres of sweet corn. In addition to their full-time workers, the Selfs would employee high school boys to help out during peak seasons. Pictured below are, from left to right, unidentified, Craig Self, unidentified, Richie Masseli, and Tommy Lacey. Bob Self is behind the wheel. (Both, courtesy of the Self family.)

Deodate Beaumont started Beaumont Farm by initially purchasing 13 acres near Maplewood Avenue and later bought the old house and additional land at the site between 1801 and 1805. The land was farmed while he ran his harness and saddle shop along with his inn, The Sign of the Saddle, on the corner of North Main and Christian Streets from 1780 to 1835. His farming operation grew and became a thriving dairy business as it passed down through multiple generations. The 5,000-square-foot barn below remains and serves as a reminder of the family farm. Deodate Beaumont served in the Revolutionary War and is buried at Center Street Cemetery. The dairy building is shown above during the 1940s. (Above, courtesy of the Wallingford Historical Society; below, courtesy of Roger Dietz.)

Coag Farm on Northford Road was started by the Cooke family in the mid-1700s. At its peak, the dairy farm operated over 1,000 acres of land and was home to 500 registered Holsteins. The farm was nationally recognized in 1988 as having been in the same family since the birth of the US Constitution. In the 1990s, Coag Farm gave up its dairy operation. Currently, the farm has 100 acres and runs a hay operation and leases a portion of its land to local vegetable and poultry producers, one of which is Muddy Roots Farm, operated by Kirstin Marra, a descendent of the Cooke family. (Both, courtesy of Roger Dietz.)

Since its founding, Wallingford agriculture has been a critical component to its success. Today, its pastoral beauty is evident in the rural landscapes, enduring family farms, and open spaces. Shown here are photographs of the Cella Brothers Farm near Whirlwind Hill and Branford Road. While many farms repurposed their land for suburban and industrial development, 82 acres of the Cella Brothers Farm was purchased by the State of Connecticut, which guarantees the land is never to be used for nonagricultural purposes. (Both, courtesy of Roger Dietz.)

Six

Manufacturing and the Silver Industry

Although Wallingford was home to a multitude of manufacturing enterprises over the centuries, the silver-plating industry was the foundation of the town's success and was born out of the craft of producing tableware out of sterling silver during the colonial years. Skilled artisans learned their trade in England or from English craftsmen who migrated to the colonies in the 17th century.

Early American silver products originated from Spanish and English coins, which were taken directly to the silversmith and melted down, creating pieces made to order. Spoons, chalices, tankards, and dram cups were popular items, and pieces like silver thimbles, shoe buckles, and hat bands were created for the wealthiest of families in New Haven and Wallingford.

Sterling products were prized possessions, often being gifted to churches and pastors within the community and bequeathed to loved ones in their wills. The last will and testament of Wallingford's Rev. Samuel Whittlesey in 1752 included 108 ounces of sterling tankards, spoons, and platters. During the British invasion of New Haven in 1779, residents attempted to conceal treasure from the plundering Redcoats. In one instance, church communion silver was hidden in a chimney in the house of Deacon Ball, which is now located on the campus of Yale University.

One of Wallingford's earliest silversmiths was Amos Doolittle, born in 1754. He was apprenticed under Eliakim Hitchcock, a Wallingford silversmith from 1750 to 1785. Doolittle's silver craft evolved to the art of engraving, and he became one of the most notable engravers in colonial history. His work, taken from personal observations, illustrated some of the most important battles of the American Revolution.

By 1800, Wallingford's population had increased to over 3,000, and Connecticut had reached over a quarter million residents. Long known for being the breadbasket of the colonies and then the "Provision State," Connecticut actively produced food and goods for times of need and times of war, and Wallingford was one of its largest contributors. Wallingford actively traded with other New England colonies, producing goods from wagon wheels to barrel hoops, buttons, beaver hats, and small metal goods and exporting over 12,000 corn brooms a year. For Wallingford, the 1800s would become a century of invention, innovation, and industrialization.

The descendants of the original colonists, with their indefatigable work ethic and enterprising ways, worked together to invest in a large variety of business ventures. Some of the first manufacturing companies could be found in the very heart of town. Elisha Pomeroy and James Kirtland produced razor strops at Center and Fair Streets while John Hall at one time was the largest producer of razor strops in the country. On South Main Street, Charles Yale began his venture into Britannia ware.

The need for more affordable housewares was recognized by Wallingford businessmen, and a new industry was formed. Sterling was not within reach of the average Wallingford citizens, and some of its most innovative residents discovered more economical alternatives, combining craftsmanship with larger scale production.

In the 1820s, Charles Yale, descendant of founder Thomas Yale, under the tutelage of English craftsmen, learned to produce a metal compound similar to pewter but less expensive. He produced a variety of hollowware, called Britannia ware, and was wildly successful, exporting his goods throughout the country.

Robert Wallace, son of a Scottish silversmith, began his career at the age of 16 as an apprentice to William Mix, a spoon maker at Meriden Britannia Company. By 1835, he purchased a gristmill in Wallingford and began the mass production of spoons made from German silver, a mixed alloy that was sturdy and economical for manufacturing on a large scale. Soon, other companies would follow. Samuel Simpson, a Wallingford native, advanced the technology of silver-plating fine metals onto more economical products like copper, steel, and tin. These items would mimic the beauty and craftsmanship of fine sterling but at an affordable price.

It was when these innovators began to master the powerful waters of the Quinnipiac River that the industry grew on a grander scale. Mills were converted to industrial plants and could be found up and down the river, producing everything from furniture to farm implements to pewter ware.

Wallingford was becoming a mecca for the silver-plate industry, and its success began to attract workers from all over New England. It also brought an influx of European immigrants who had fled their countries over political upheavals, economic hardships, and poverty. These workers found a home in Wallingford, bringing new skills and artistic talent and traditions to the community. The industry provided many of these skilled craftsmen an opportunity to advance and gain entrance into managerial positions.

By the middle of the 1800s, manufacturing was in full swing. Thousands of workers were employed in the production of hollowware (vases, cups, and bowls) and flatware. The facilities were growing enormous in size and were now using water and steam to power the factories. With the creation of the patent system in Connecticut in 1790, hundreds of patents were issued to Wallingford and Meriden industrialists throughout the 1800s in recognition of the improvements in manufacturing and innovative designs in the industry.

While Wallingford's first foray into the metal industry was manufacturing utilitarian items, this grew to include artful designs that were exported all over the world, and their products were considered specimens of American ingenuity and skill. Wallingford manufacturers embraced the aesthetic movement of the 19th century and employed artists from Europe to produce silverware and tableware that was embellished and rich in detail. Their work was considered a part of the fine arts movement and was displayed at trade shows and exhibitions around the world, often receiving medals of honor.

Eventually, the silver industry in Wallingford began to face economic downturns, and smaller companies merged into one, forming the International Silver Company. Robert Wallace's empire changed hands several times over the decades yet continues to produce highly prized flatware under the name Wallace Silversmiths Inc.

Robert Wallace was born in 1815 in Prospect, Connecticut. He was the son of James Wallace, a Scottish immigrant and silversmith. In 1831, Robert Wallace began apprenticing for William Mix, a maker of pewter goods for the Meriden Britannia Company, and learned the art of silver craft. He opened his own shop making spoons and began contracting out work for various manufacturers in Wallingford. After stumbling upon a nickel alloy that was found to be sturdy yet economical for spoon making, he brought the formula to Wallingford and began producing spoons with Hall, Elton & Company. Over the years, Wallace formed several companies in the cutlery and hollowware industry, partnering with Samuel Simpson in Wallace, Simpson & Son in 1865. He would eventually form R. Wallace and Son's Manufacturing Company in 1871 and add sterling silver items to his production line. Wallace died in 1892 in Wallingford and was regarded as a great philanthropist within the community.

Robert Wallace's silver industry grew from simple spoons to a multi-corporate industry by the end of the 19th century, employing hundreds of workers of varied skills. Employment included modelers, chasers, spinners, blank cutters, trimmers, buffers, engravers, polishers, and floor supervisors (pictured above). Administration workers included bookkeepers and traveling sales staff. It was said that Robert Wallace, president of the Wallace empire, spent little time in the administrative offices and was often found in his apron, sitting at his work bench in the factory with his men. By 1893, the Wallace factory in Wallingford had over 600 employees and showrooms in New York and Chicago. The main factory building in Wallingford also produced solid silver products, and the first floor housed a large fireproof vault, where the company secured its silver bullion. When the administration building was constructed at 340 Quinnipiac Street in the early 1920s, it included hot water, a ventilation system, and separate reading and lunchrooms for men and women workers. It was a far cry from the horse-powered plants of the mid-19th century.

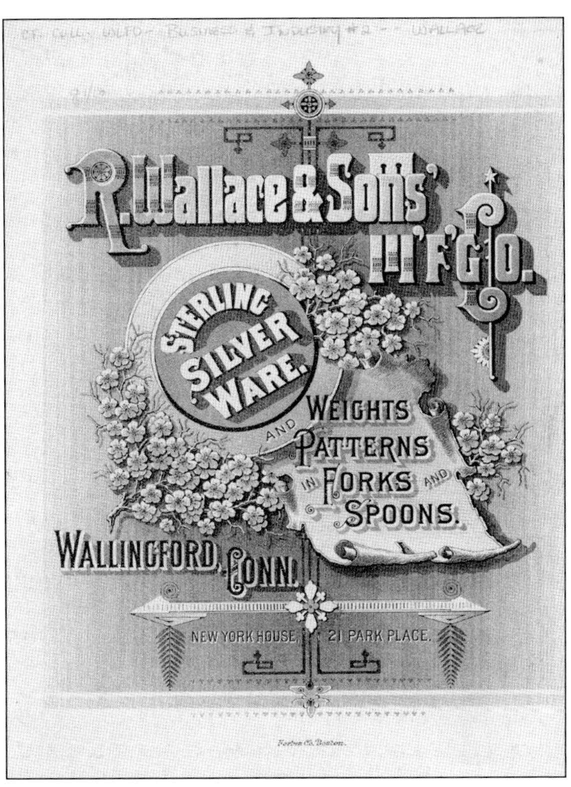

Manufacturers employed fine artists to produce beautifully illustrated catalogs detailing their wares. By the middle of the 19th century, tableware lines grew more elaborate, as did the style of the Victorian era. The Wallace companies additionally published a guideline for the consumer, instructing them on how to set the "perfect" table. They also carried a line of wedding silver and souvenir spoons, and in 1893, Wallace's companies produced separate lines of silver tableware specifically for hotels and steamships. Samuel Simpson and Robert Wallace each had showrooms in New York City and Chicago.

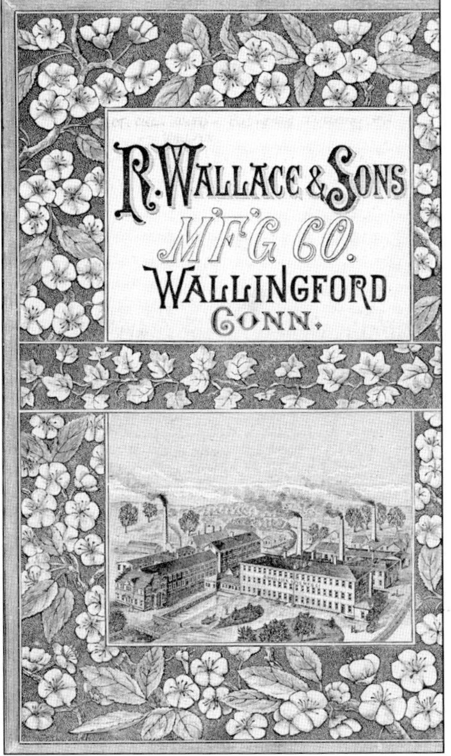

Samuel Simpson, born in 1814, was best known for his advancements in the silver-plating and Britannia ware industry. He began his career as an apprentice to Charles Yale, who produced Britannia ware in Wallingford under the name of Meriden Britannia Company. After rising to foreman, Samuel Simpson purchased the company and introduced an innovative process of electroplating silver onto metal housewares. Simpson sold his interest in the Meriden Britannia Company and partnered with several associates to form Wallace, Simpson & Company and Simpson, Hall, Miller & Company. In the 1860s, he employed hundreds of Wallingford residents in his factories and offices.

Pictured above are administration workers at Factory L at the Simpson, Hall, Miller & Company. In 1898, Simpson, Hall, Miller & Company was absorbed into the International Silver Company. In the early 20th century, local silver workers joined other manufacturing employees throughout New England on a massive strike to unionize. During the strike wave of the summer of 1915, silver buffers were rated at 18¢ per hour, and females were paid 7¢ per hour. Their days were long, laboring 10-hour shifts for 60 hours a week. The International Silver Company employees joined over 8,000 workers throughout Connecticut to fight for shorter workdays and fair wages. The women fought for a minimum wage of $8 a week. Wallingford and Meriden citizens pulled together to help support the workers and their efforts. In one notable event, International Silver Company's Factory H manager, George Munson, imported two truckloads of professional strikebreakers and incited one of the first riots in the strike, resulting in bricks being thrown and glass broken throughout the plant. In addition to intimidating workers with taunts and threatening them with weapons, hot water was streamed at the strikers and shots were fired. By August 1915, most of the labor disputes were settled, and the shorter workday was won for most workers. (Both, courtesy of the Wallingford Historical Society.)

Employees are pictured at Factory L at Simpson, Hall, Miller & Company around 1890. (Courtesy of the Wallingford Historical Society.)

Samuel Simpson founded Simpson, Hall, Miller & Company at the end of the Civil War in 1866. He operated his manufacturing plant on Simpson's Pond, on the east side of Wallingford, and produced a wide variety of electroplated silver products for the home. A dam on Simpson's Pond is shown here. (Courtesy of the Wallingford Historical Society.)

Charles Henry Tibbits (pictured at right with his son Charles and father, William, and below) was born in 1866 in West Plains, New York. After graduating from Trinity College, he taught Latin for two years in Waterbury, Connecticut. Soon after, he became a salesman at the New York store for Simpson, Hall, Miller & Company, rising to an administrative position soon after. He was appointed secretary of the Simpson Nickel Company. In 1891, he married Georgiana Hull, granddaughter to company owner Samuel Simpson, and when Samuel Simpson died in 1894, Tibbits helped steady the ship. In 1898, all of Simpson's silver manufacturing companies merged with the International Silver Company, and Tibbitts became third vice president of the merger. He carried on managing two of the company's factories in Wallingford. He served as Wallingford's electric commissioner for years, and in 1919, formed the Tibbits and Tabor Company, manufacturing silver goods with his son-in-law. (Both, courtesy of Robert A. Taber.)

Gurdon Hull was born in Wallingford in 1834. At the age of 16, he was apprenticed to spoon manufacturer William Mix. In 1866, he became an investor in Simpson, Hall, Miller & Company, where he was also a designer, receiving patents in the later part of the 1800s for spoons and table service ware. Later, Hull was charged with the business affairs of the New York City operation. He was married to Samuel Simpson's daughter Elizabeth in 1864 and was father to Elizabeth Hull Manning and Georgiana Hull Tibbits. Hull's death in New York City in May 1894 one month after the death of his father-in-law Samuel Simpson was a devastating loss to the family and to Simpson's manufacturing interests. Within four years of their deaths, the Simpson manufacturing companies would merge into the International Silver Company. (Courtesy of the Wallingford Historical Society.)

William Elton was born in 1811 in Burlington, Connecticut. In his early 20s, he partnered with Wallingford's Lemuel Curtis to form Curtis and Hall Company, manufacturing spoons in Wallingford. From 1847 to 1865, he was partners with Almer Hall and Jacob Hall and formed Hall, Elton & Company, manufacturing flatware in German silver. The company first had a factory on the Quinnipiac River but moved its operation to Hall Avenue, where its building still stands today. Hall, Elton & Company was issued multiple patents during the 19th century, including one for an improvement in die cutting for spoon blanks. The company exhibited its work throughout the country, including at the Centennial International Exposition of 1876 in Philadelphia. (Courtesy of the Wallingford Historical Society.)

Charles Parker was born in Cheshire in 1809. He began his career in manufacturing as a pewter button maker in Southington, Connecticut. With $70 saved, he began his own business in 1829 and was contracted to produce coffee mills. He began with a small shop and only three employees. By 1870, he had 16 manufacturing plants in Meriden and Yalesville and was producing an enormous variety of goods. He began with coffee mills, but production expanded to piano stools, tobacco boxes, and double-barrel shotguns. Above, the Charles Parker Company plant in Meriden is pictured. Below are some of the company's employees around 1890.

Interior photographs of the Charles Parker Company factory show the complicated tangle of pulleys used to manufacture items. Charles Parker was one of the first industrialists to bring steam power into manufacturing in Meriden. He expanded his enterprise to include metal works like brass hardware. He established the Meriden Curtain Fixture Company, which made decorative items for the home. These products were exhibited throughout the country, including at the Centennial International Exposition of 1876 in Philadelphia and the 1893 World's Columbian Exposition in Chicago, where they were awarded for their beauty and functionality. Today, Parker Art Brass designs are sought after and collectible and can be found in museums and galleries throughout the country.

Floyd Wallace Sr., above left, was the grandson of Robert Wallace, founder of the Wallace silver empire, and son of Frank A. Wallace. When Robert Wallace died in 1892, his sons took over R. Wallace and Sons Manufacturing Company, naming Frank A. Wallace as president. By 1893, the company employed over 600 people and continued to manufacture silver products for decades, becoming the largest tableware producers in the world. Their companies included R. Wallace and Sons Manufacturing Company and Wallace Silversmiths. The Wallace descendants continued in the business, adding new lines of products and securing large contracts to provide silverware to steamships and railroad service. Mass production was improved, and the company implemented the most modern of manufacturing practices. Shown below is the Wallace Silversmiths sales force in 1940, a far cry from the early days when spoons were sold by peddlers traveling by horse and buggy.

R. Wallace and Sons Manufacturing Company also produced a variety of objects besides flatware in the late 1800s and early 1900s. The need for highly ornamental designs created a distinct branch of art within the silver-manufacturing industry, employing dozens of skilled artists who were constantly seeking to create new patterns. The silver-plated match safes, right, were produced around 1900 in the classic Art Nouveau style. Below, the illustration of a julep spoon represents one of many Victorian barware designs produced by R. Wallace and Sons Manufacturing Company. The julep spoon was designed as a strainer and was to remain in the cocktail glass after serving. R. Wallace and Sons Manufacturing Company products are highly prized and collected throughout the world and have been exhibited at the Metropolitan Museum of Art in New York City.

STERLING MATCH BOXES

French Gray. Splendid examples of workmanship, and appropriate to the time of the year, for those who swore off smoking January first are about due to backslide now

From left to right — No. 872; No. 870; No. 884
2⅝ inches high

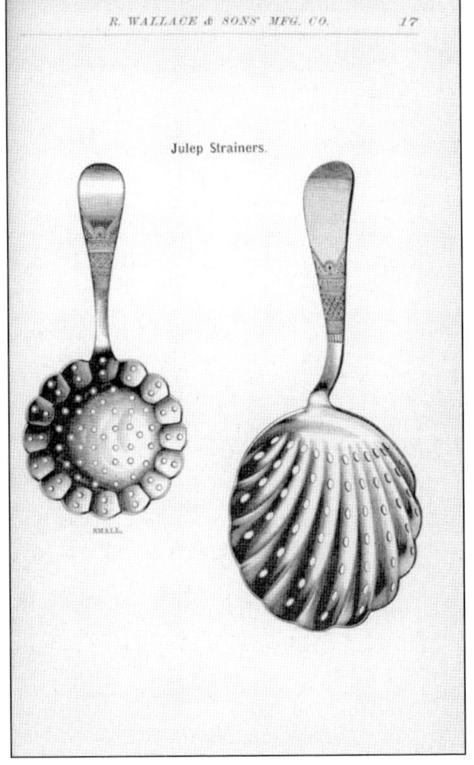

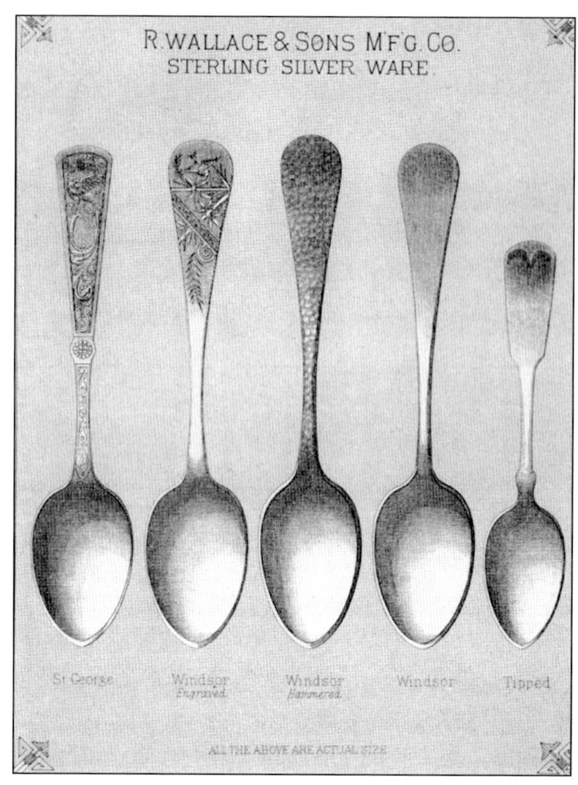

R. Wallace and Sons Manufacturing Company was formed in 1879 and produced a wide range of sterling silver and silver-plated flatware and cutlery. The illustrations left and below represent several of the R. Wallace and Sons 19th-century spoon patterns. The St. George, far left, has an embossed dragon, which represented the dragon slain by St. George. The company's spoon designs ranged from plain ornamentation to highly decorative patterns.

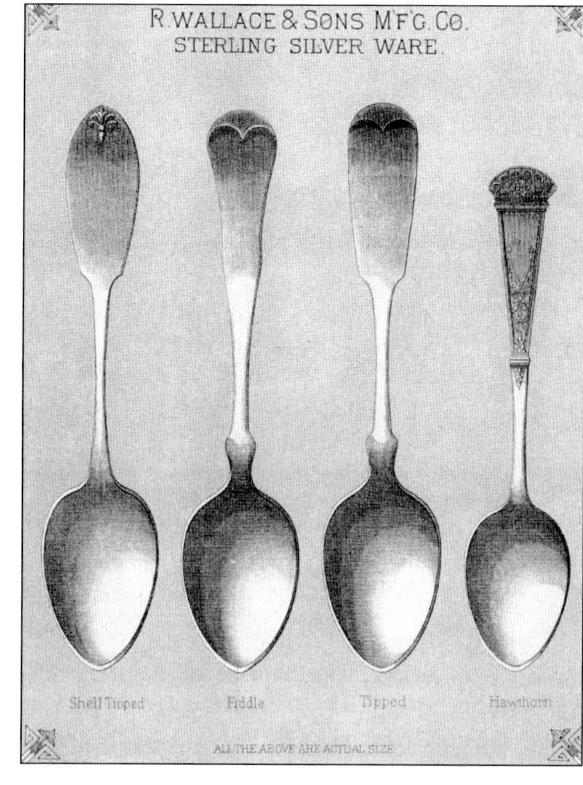

At the turn of the 20th century, one of R. Wallace and Sons Manufacturing Company's chief silver designers was Henrik Hillbom, shown here with his wife. His artistic career began in Sweden. He was born in 1863 in Uppsala County and showed an early talent for painting and crafts. When he was 18, he studied the art of goldsmithing and design at the Technical Institute in Stockholm. In 1890, Hillbom studied at the Académie Julian in Paris. He was a member of the Society of Independent Artists, the Hartford Salmagundi Art Club, and the New Haven Paint and Clay Club. He also became part of the Old Lyme Art Colony in Lyme, Connecticut. (Courtesy of the Wallingford Historic Preservation Trust.)

After Hillbom's death, sculptor Edward Widstrom created a bust of the artist that was exhibited in New York City in 1973. Widstrom was a designer for the International Silver Company and a fellow at the National Sculpture Society. The bust is on display at the Franklin Johnson Museum on South Main Street. (Courtesy of Roger Dietz.)

In 1900, Henrik Hillbom began his career as a designer in the chasing and engraving department at R. Wallace and Sons Manufacturing Company. One of his first designs was a flatware handle pattern named "Violet" (shown above), which was given a US patent in 1904. He also designed the patterns "Berain," "Carnation," "Irian," and "Lady Windsor." Hillbom continued to produce stunning ornamental designs for the company and was eventually promoted to head of design. (Both, courtesy of the Wallingford Historic Preservation Trust.)

William S. Warren was born in 1888 in England and came to the United States at the age of nine. He was a master designer and sculpture for R. Wallace and Sons Manufacturing Company from 1909 to 1959. He attended the Industrial School of Art in Philadelphia and held an apprenticeship at Tiffany and Company before joining R. Wallace and Sons. (Courtesy of Bob Beaumont.)

From 1934 to 1950, R. Wallace and Sons Manufacturing Company released its most famous line of sterling flatware called Third Dimensional Beauty Collection, which earned patents for design and mechanics. The "Rose Point" pattern, seen here, was released in 1934 and was one of the early collection patterns. The "Grande Baroque" pattern was also designed by William S. Warren in 1941 and included over 500 pieces in the collection. Today, Warren's sterling flatware is highly collectable. (Courtesy of Bob Beaumont.)

The New York Insulated Wire Company mill was first built in 1883 by the Wilson Sewing Machine Company of Chicago. When that business failed after two years, the Metropolitan Rubber Company, manufacturers of rubber clothing, and the New York Insulated Wire Company moved in, supplying wire to the telegraph and telephone companies. They occupied the mill until the 1920s. The building, which has been repurposed several times, was used as a knitting factory and for the manufacture of apparel, and now serves as residential apartments.

Morton Judd founded the Judd Manufacturing Company in 1830, manufacturing metalworks. The company was moved from New Haven to Wallingford, where it employed over 1,000 hands, including skilled artisans, in the production of decorative arts such as bookends and metal mechanical banks, which are highly collectible today. The company was later taken over by Morton Judd's sons. When Hubert Judd died in 1899, he was one of the wealthiest men in Wallingford and resided in a large mansion on South Main Street.

In 1851, a religious group from Oneida, New York, relocated to a 250-acre farm along the Quinnipiac River, one mile west of Wallingford center. At first employing only 50 people, they farmed the land, growing strawberries and fruits to support their small commune. Eventually they constructed a dam across the Quinnipiac River, creating Community Lake, seen here. With the waters of the Quinnipiac powering their factory, they began producing steel animal traps and later plated tin flatware, adding to Wallingford's extensive manufacturing industry. The company transferred its manufacturing back to Oneida, New York, in 1880, and still produces flatware today under the name of Oneida Ltd. Community Lake was enjoyed by Wallingford residents for another 100 years for recreational purposes and served as the practice location for the Choate Rosemary Hall rowing team. The dam failed in 1979, and the lake dried up, leaving a lake bed of 75 acres.

Seven

Honoring and Preserving

One of Wallingford's remarkable characteristics is the preservation of the histories and memories of its earliest days. Since Wallingford's very first year as a fledgling plantation, clerks kept careful records of the day-to-day transactions of the town that have served to illustrate life in early Wallingford. Town leaders and clerics understood the significance of record keeping and the importance it would have to future generations. Land transactions, wills, testaments, and extensive genealogies that explore Wallingford's oldest families all give a glimpse into Wallingford's colonial life.

Although Rev. James Dana wrote the first history of Wallingford in 1770, a more comprehensive effort was made 100 years later. In 1870, Charles Henry Davis (1840–1917), a Wallingford native, decided to take on the monumental task of sifting through thousands of pages of town records dating back to the first weeks of the new plantation. Drawing from ancient records of the New Haven and Connecticut Colonies, he began to piece together the history of Wallingford. He conducted interviews with the oldest of the town's inhabitants and gathered genealogical records of the descendants of the founding fathers. His hard work and perseverance resulted in the publication of *History of Wallingford, Connecticut: From Its Settlement in 1670 to the Present Time, Including Meriden, which was One of Its Parishes Until 1806, and Cheshire, which was Incorporated in 1780*, published in 1870 by the author and printed locally by Wallingford's Mount Tom Printing House. The book is available from the Wallingford Public Library and online. In addition, various Wallingford histories used in the preparation of this book are available from the Wallingford Public Library's Connecticut Collection.

The Yale family name has been rooted in Wallingford history since the first Yale set foot in the New Haven Colony in the 17th century. Anne Yale, widow of Thomas Yale, came from England to New Haven. Their grandson Thomas Yale was an original founder of Wallingford. The Yale family's story reaches far beyond the towns of New Haven and Wallingford, and their descendants include notable artists and writers such as Norman Rockwell, Henry Wadsworth Longfellow, and Ernest Hemingway.

Another notable descendent of Wallingford is British prime minister Winston Churchill (1940–1945 and 1951–1955). His ancestral roots in Wallingford are through his maternal lineage. Churchill's mother, Jennie Jerome, is a direct descendent of Samuel Jerome, who was born in Wallingford in 1728. That makes Wallingford colonist Samuel Jerome Winston Churchill's great-great-great-grandfather.

The Hall family is one of the more prolific families of Wallingford. Their roots stretch back to the colonial era, with each generation entwining their branches with other notable Wallingford names, such as Doolittle, Whittlesey, Royce, and Atwater.

The Halls produced copious amounts of children, often christening them with the names of the beloved ancestors who came before them. The Hon. John Hall Sr., son of Samuel and grandson of the first John Hall, was born in 1693. His children include Eliakim Hall, colonel in the French and Indian War and the Revolutionary War, and John Hall (born in 1693), who was the father of Lyman, Giles, and Colonel Street Hall.

The Halls continued to prosper, leaving scores of descendants to carry on for another 340 years. Several reminders of the Halls during colonial times still exist. The sword once belonging to Eliakim Hall resides at the Smithsonian Institution. The Giles Hall House on South Elm Street is one of the handful of colonial-era homes still standing in Wallingford, Lyman Hall is memorialized throughout Wallingford as a signer of the Declaration of Independence, and the names of scores of Halls who gave their lives to the country are etched upon town monuments.

The commitment to preserving the past remains a passion of Wallingford historians and is shared with the citizenry through celebrations and memorials. Enthusiastic support for honoring past leaders, heroes, and events continues today and can be attributed to a deep connection to the foundations set forth 350 years ago. The ties that bind Wallingford together and the freedoms that are held dear are clearly defined by the continued and expanding worship community, an innovative and inclusive education community, strong and adaptable business and farming communities, and committed and responsive government leadership. In addition, arts, recreation, and leisure activities have grown and become vital elements in positioning Wallingford to embrace a future of prosperity and continued growth.

A walk through Center Street Cemetery is like walking through Wallingford's past. Elaborate headstones and monuments as well as simple stones and slabs mark the lives of many of Wallingford's citizens who helped shaped the town, state, and country. The Center Street Cemetery, although formally established in 1683, has been an active burial ground for 350 years and includes the remains of Wallingford's earliest settlers, including both prominent leaders and common citizens. Some notable persons interred here include founding father John Moss, who died in 1707 at the age of 103, and Abraham Doolittle, who died in 1690 at age 70 and was a prominent citizen who served as a town selectman and as a member of the general court. His home was one of those fortified against Indian attacks in the early days of the town. Rev. Samuel Street, first pastor of First Church, is also at rest here, having died in 1717 at the age of 82. Wallingford citizens who served in the Revolutionary War, French and Indian War, Civil War, World War I, World War II, the Korean War, the Vietnam War, and many other conflicts are interred here. (Courtesy of William Burgess.)

Founded in 1916, the Wallingford Historical Society was formed to gather, protect, and preserve the history of Wallingford. The first president and vice president of the society were Marshall K. Thomas and Judge John Phelan, respectively. Both historians had written several journals and articles detailing the lives of Wallingford's earliest settlers. They implored citizens to contribute family papers, diaries, Bibles, and scrapbooks for future generations. By 1920, the Historical House, as it was then known, began opening to the public each Sunday. It was in the 1930s that the society began its tradition of educating Wallingford schoolchildren, conducting tours of the museum and teaching them about the daily lives of their colonial ancestors. The citizens of Wallingford have generously contributed toward acquisitions of artifacts and the funds to help improve the Samuel Parsons house and its upkeep. The Wallingford Historical Society considers its outreach program to Wallingford children one of its most important accomplishments. It continues the 80-year tradition of providing tours to hundreds of Wallingford third graders each year, hoping to spark within them a love of history. The society also holds several exhibits throughout the year. For those with an interest in military artifacts, there is an impressive collection of antique uniforms, helmets, and battle dress. (Courtesy of the Wallingford Historical Society.)

Fannie Ives Schember, benefactor of the Wallingford Historical Society, was born in 1842 to Eli S. Ives, a Wallingford probate judge, and Lodema Delight Thompson. She is a descendant of William Ives, an original founder of the New Haven Colony. Her ancestry is dotted with the old Wallingford family names of Silliman, Parker, and Jerome. As the granddaughter of 19th-century carriage and coffin maker Capt. Caleb Thompson, she spent much of her early years at his home. The charming Dutch Colonial was built in 1759 and became known as the Samuel Parsons House. In the late 1700s, it was used as a tavern, catering to stagecoaches traveling the old Post Road between Boston and New York City. Fannie Schember inherited the home, which had been in her family since 1803. When the Wallingford Historical Society outgrew its home in the turret of the former Judd Mansion on South Main Street, Schember deeded her home to the society in 1919, retaining life use of it. In 1930, upon her demise, the historical society became owner of the Samuel Parsons House, in fee simple. In addition, many of the early furniture items on display in the home came from her estate. (Courtesy of the Wallingford Historical Society.)

The Nehemiah Royce House was built in the 17th century at the north end of the Long Highway by Nehemiah Royce and his brothers. It stands as one of the oldest houses in Wallingford and is a wonderful example of colonial saltbox architecture. Distinctive reminders of Nehemiah Royce and his brothers remain in the house. The initial "R" is etched on the latch of an old door, and a giant millstone from the Royce family gristmill sits outside the front door, now serving as a steppingstone into the home's main entrance. The home stayed in the Royce family for generations. After descendant Helen Royce's death, the house was donated to the Society of New England Antiquities. It was then donated to Choate Rosemary Hall in 1962. In 1999, the house was donated to the Wallingford Historic Preservation Trust, founded in 1991 by local historian Jerry Farrell Jr. with the primary objective of preserving Wallingford architectural and cultural heritage. The trust provides education to residents, schools, and visitors through demonstrating common colonial trades such as blacksmithing, weaving, and spinning. It also provide tours of downtown Wallingford, based on historic citizens' early businesses, and distinguished architecture, both past and present. (Courtesy of the Wallingford Historical Society.)

The Franklin Johnson House at 153 South Main Street was built in 1866 for Franklin Johnson, a successful farmer and Wallingford businessman. Johnson sold a portion of his land, which was located where Ashlar Village now stands, to his son Homer Johnson. He used the proceeds to purchase the property on South Main Street and built the 2.5-story Italianate mansion. Franklin Johnson was the great-great-great-grandson of William Johnson, signer of the original Wallingford Covenant. Franklin Johnson was a town selectman and one of the founders of the First Baptist Church. The mansion was restored by the Wallingford Historic Preservation Trust in the late 1990s. It was listed in the National Register of Historic Places in 1998 and serves as the American Silver Museum. (Courtesy of the Wallingford Historic Preservation Trust.)

Choate Rosemary Hall, a private college preparatory boarding school, is in the center of Wallingford and is considered a gem within the community. Rosemary Hall was founded in 1890 by Mary Atwater Choate, great-granddaughter of Caleb Atwater, and her husband, William Gardner Choate, on Rosemary Farm in Wallingford. They later founded Choate School, a private boy's boarding school, in 1896. One of the many historic homes on this prestigious campus is the Squire Oliver Stanley House at 166 Christian Street. Built between 1690 and 1750, it was originally known as the Red House. Oliver Stanley Esq. was a captain in the Revolutionary War and later a member of the General Assembly. When Gen. George Washington rode through Wallingford in 1775, he took tea with Oliver Stanley at the Red House. The Red House became the residence of the first class of the boy's school under the tutelage of Mark Pitman. Today, the Choate Rosemary Hall campus covers 458 acres and maintains and preserves a wide variety of architectural structures, from 18th-century homes, which are used as campus residences, to classic Georgian Revival buildings and magnificent modern structures designed by I.M. Pei and James Polshek. (Courtesy of the Wallingford Historical Society.)

George Washington made two notable appearances in Wallingford. In 1775, on his way from the Second Continental Congress to take charge of the Continental army in Concord, he stopped at Caleb Atwater's store for gunpowder. He then stopped at Nehemiah Royce's home, where he addressed the citizens under a huge elm tree on Royce's property. Because of this extraordinary visit, the Royces' house came to be known as the Washington Elm House. His second trip through town was in 1789, shortly after his presidential inauguration. In 1932, Wallingford participated in a nationwide celebration of the 200th anniversary of Washington's birth and formed its own George Washington Bicentennial Commission to commemorate President Washington's visits through Wallingford in 1775 and 1789. Six markers were installed from east of Wallace Avenue to Washington Trail and finally to the foot of Tri-Mountain, the location being known as "Great Gate." Ostensibly these first six markers were installed by October 19, 1932, in time for the citizens to follow Levi Morelle Cooke, riding a horse and dressed as George Washington, along the route to Durham. (Courtesy of William Burgess.)

On the north side of Cheshire Road is a park dedicated to Maj. Gervais Raoul Lufbery. He was, at one time, a household name thanks to his exploits as an airman in World War I. Born in France, Lufbery lived in Wallingford and worked at a silver-manufacturing factory prior to his joining the war effort in the Lafayette Escadrille and the US Air Service. He became a noted American air ace in October 1916 after downing his fifth enemy aircraft. He died in May 1918 when his aircraft was shot down in France. Lufbery was awarded the Purple Heart for his sacrifice. Commemorating servicemen exemplifies Wallingford's patriotism. Shown below is the Civil War Circle at Center Street Cemetery. This memorial is dedicated to the 19 Wallingford soldiers who gave their lives during the Civil War. (Left, courtesy of the Wallingford Historical Society; below, courtesy of the Wallingford Historic Preservation Trust.)

Wallingford's Abraham Doolittle, born in 1620, was the progenitor of the Doolittle family in America. He came from England to Boston, eventually landing in the New Haven Colony in 1642. Abraham Doolittle became one of the founding members of Wallingford, holding several positions of importance. He was first appointed to look after the affairs of the new Wallingford plantation, then assigned surveyor of highways in 1673. He was also a member of the Vigilance Committee during King Philip's War. After the death of his first wife, he married Abigail Moss, the daughter of John Moss, who was also one of the signers of the original plantation covenant. Abraham Doolittle was the father of 13 children and over the centuries was responsible for a line of descendants that now reach from coast to coast. Stillman Doolittle, who had lived on Pond Hill Road, left funds for the purchase of suitable land for a park. At the time of its purchase, the park was 15 acres and the largest in town. In 1931, Doolittle Park was opened on South Elm Street. In the 1940s, Wharton Brook was dammed to create an outdoor skating area east of the utility building, with ball fields and tennis courts to the west.

Community organizations are a stalwart in the town of Wallingford, and the Wallingford Grange is no exception. Wallingford Grange Hall No. 33 at 585 Center Street was founded in 1885 by William Ellsworth Hall and Marcus E. Cooke. Its intent was to educate, support, and promote the agricultural society of Wallingford. It continues to serve with acts of community service, family activities, programs, and contests designed to promote leadership and support for the educational, legislative, and business interests of the agricultural community. Wallingford citizens have long come together in support of common interests. In 1918, there were well over 40 fraternal societies, clubs, and similar organizations in town, each defining a mission for the betterment of specific interests. As the community evolved, old organizations changed with the times and new organizations developed. Masons, Odd Fellows, Knights of Columbus, temperance societies, ethnic clubs, youth clubs, and many more are a part of Wallingford's community history. Seniors, ethnic communities, and business communities are all represented in a variety of clubs and organizations in present-day Wallingford. With the support of the town's Park and Recreation Department, a multitude of opportunities are available to all ages who seek to develop their interests in sports, arts, and exercise.

The tradition of contests and celebrations to commemorate significant events in Wallingford history is exemplified by the Wallingford tercentenary celebration of 1970 and the crowning of Joan Pashley as the Jubilee 300 queen. As winner of the Jubilee 300 contest, Pashley was awarded a two-week trip for two to England, including flights, lodging, and car rental. In addition, she received $200 in expense money, Napier jewelry, a wristwatch, silver service for eight from the International Silver Company, a color portrait, a wig, and Lady Clairol beauty set. Nearly 30 women competed for the honor and prizes were awarded to first, second, third, and fourth princesses. Just a couple years later in 1972, a contest for young women began as a way to promote interest in sports among high school girls, and the Wallingford Powderpuff flag football rivalry between Lyman Hall High School and Mark T. Sheehan High School was born. Now called the Samaha Bowl after its creator, former Sheehan High School athletic director Judy Samaha, it is traditionally played the day before Thanksgiving. It is the longest-running powderpuff football game in the nation and is attended by thousands of spectators, second only to the crowd that attends Wallingford fireworks each year to celebrate the Fourth of July.

Celebrations of historic and patriotic events are important elements of Wallingford's culture. Following a Fourth of July parade on North Main Street in the 1920s, a fife and drum corps dressed in colonial garb poses for a photograph. Each year, the Wallingford Historical Society holds a Fourth of July picnic and ceremoniously rings the old town hall bell, which was cast in 1869 and donated to the society in 1963. In the early 1970s, Wallingford was part of a national effort to plan events and celebrations to commemorate the nation's 200th birthday. One of the enduring and beloved results of this planning was the founding of the Wallingford Symphony Orchestra. Founded in 1974 by Wallingford's Bicentennial Commission, in conjunction with Choate Rosemary Hall, each year the symphony provides a free concert as part of the Fourth of July celebrations. Commemorating and honoring military men and women who have lost their lives in service to the country, the Wallingford Veterans Memorial Committee organizes the Memorial Day Parade. Celebrations produced by the town's celebration committee, programs and events produced by Wallingford Center Inc., and beautification projects and the efforts of the Wallingford Garden Club are just some of the important examples that showcase Wallingford's respect for the past and excitement for the future.

Forged out of wilderness, the colonial plantation of Wallingford developed into a sleepy little New England village and then into a vibrant town at the crossroads of major modern thoroughfares. All through its growth however, elements of its rural past are preserved in designated parks, protected open spaces, and bucolic landscapes. This photograph of a boy fishing at North Farms Reservoir evokes contemplation, perhaps a reflection on the past or hope for the future. In either case, Wallingford is poised to continue honoring the explorers and adventurers of the 17th century while meeting the demands of an evolving 21st-century community. Referencing the Davis history of Wallingford and the author's observation about recorded history: "Our nation owes a lasting debt of gratitude to our ancestors for their fidelity in recording the incipient steps taken by them in settling this new world." And so, the citizens of Wallingford have a lasting debt to the men and women who came before and endured. Their foresight in leaving New Haven and adventuring northward has given great cause for celebrating Wallingford's 350th anniversary.